8.20.09

To Write on Tamara?

To Write on Tamara?

Marcel Bénabou

Écrire sur Tamara

TRANSLATED BY STEVEN RENDALL

University of Nebraska Press : Lincoln and London

Publication of this translation was assisted
by a grant from the French Ministry
of Culture — National Center for the Book.

Library of Congress Cataloging-in-Publication Data
Bénabou, Marcel.
[Ecrire sur Tamara. English]
To write on Tamara / Marcel Bénabou ; translated
by Steven Rendall.
p. cm.
ISBN 0-8032-1336-0 (cl : alk. paper) – ISBN 0-8032-6215-9
(pbk. : alk. paper)
I. Rendall, Steven. II. Title.
PQ2662.E4714E2513 2004 843'.914–dc22 2003061330

CONTENTS

To Write on Tamara?

The one who rises and never stops,
moving from beginnings to beginnings
by never-ending beginnings.

Gregory of Nyssa

Preamble

To write on Tamara? Perhaps I would rather say: not to write on her. And consider myself released, once and for all, from the commitment I made long ago. For although I've been trying to fulfill that commitment for more than thirty years, my efforts, with slight variations, have always followed the same course.

First, a long period of voluntary abstention. Months and months go by, during which I forbid myself to write anything at all relating to my friend's story, which nonetheless haunts me. A constraint resolutely accepted, the benefits of which I'm sure I'll be able to reap in the long run.

And then one fine evening (it always happens in the evening, or even in the middle of the night), without warning, the reward I've been waiting for arrives: I suddenly perceive – unfolding itself as a whole before my eyes, organized down to its smallest articulations – my book! Everything is in place: not only the characters, the events, the settings, the feelings, but also the words, the sentences, the paragraphs. As if some magic grid secretly determined its rigorous structure. A vision that explodes at the surface of my consciousness, as real, as precise, as familiar as my own image in the mirror every morning.

Dazzled, I immediately get out of bed and dash, like one obsessed, to get my pen.

But then – how often I've had this experience! – there is, every time, the breakdown. None of what I've had so clearly and precisely before my eyes an instant earlier, none of what I was preparing myself piously to collect and transcribe, wants to reappear: in a flash, my book has vanished into the abyss. An insurmountable terror has completely annihilated it, leaving me with nothing but a great, embarrassed silence.

3

Then there's nothing I can do but lay down my pen. And wait. Once again, I will have to be content, for a few more months, a few more years perhaps, to write Tamara's story only in my dreams.

Sometimes, however, a few bits of debris remain floating on the surface, and after many efforts I manage to fish them out. Then I see appearing on my paper, by fits and starts, compact groups of sentences that take the most diverse forms: recapitulative notes, injunctions addressed to myself, snatches of a novel, passages of introspective analysis. Pages that do not, of course, satisfy me, and that in my rage I'm immediately ready to strike out. I don't destroy them all, however. As a sort of superstition, I always keep a few. I imagine that they might be useful someday, either as first-hand testimony on certain key moments in my life, or as fragments of the diary I've always hesitated to write.

These pages are the ones I now want to use to construct my narrative. I've put myself in the position of a person who sets out to publish the last, unfinished work of a dead friend. You know, reader, how people proceed in such a case: they search, in the mass of papers left by the deceased, for something that will help them determine the author's precise intentions; they discover, or reconstitute as nearly as possible, the structure of the work; they set in place, exactly where the author had intended them to be, the pieces that seem finished; then they try, as best they can, to situate those for which no place had yet been assigned; finally, they write the linking passages that seem indispensable for moving from one document to another. A rigorous procedure, which I shall adopt, but which I am not sure I can sustain to the end. For whereas, in the model I've chosen, the obliging friend acts without being himself engaged in the pages he's dealing with, and can thus carry out his work of assemblage as a philologist, my position is completely different. Each fragment I touch immediately touches me in return. Because these pages written in my hand always contain a bit of my own memory. Because they are also parts of a thick dossier, that of the case I'm building against myself for not having been able, at the threshold of my adult life, to persuade the woman I loved to share my love.

And it matters little if these pages seem naïve to some people, and well suited to confirm André Gide's remarks about the supposed link between good sentiments and bad literature. That is a risk I accept, and it even seems to me to have a certain usefulness, for in this risk I find the indispensable "bull's horn."[1] Everyone now knows that, like the strange ingredients formerly used in many a witch's brew (such as toad's saliva, scorpion's foot, or viper's liver), the hard and conical member that grows on the head of certain ruminants (the art of the *torero* consists in knowing how to sidestep it gracefully) is supposed to possess a rather rare virtue: that of defending against the accusation of complacency those who engage in confessional literature.

1

Arrival

At first, he saw only the gates. High. Close-set. Pointed. Brutally thrusting upon his eyes the obstacle of their steely rigidity. So that he saw virtually nothing of the dirty, almost black building that loomed behind them; the autumn mist had absorbed its contours.

Macabre? Lugubrious? Sinister? Funereal? Sepulchral? He quickly gave up searching his mind for the most appropriate adjective. The little interior voice to which he had entrusted the task of transforming into words or bookish phrases each of the new experiences that were infallibly going to enrich him was suddenly struck dumb. This auxiliary, without which he thought himself incapable of perceiving anything, had apparently given up. Still, what experience could be more novel than the one he was having at that instant: his first encounter with the establishment in which he was going to be confined for an unforeseeable length of time? But it was an experience for which he hadn't had time to prepare himself, and this moment he had so long anticipated took him by surprise. So many unexpected things had happened since he'd given his sister, on the port of Casablanca's dock no. 3, a long farewell kiss.

First of all—right after the excessively meticulous formalities connected with the police and customs, which had annoyed him— there was the very special sort of hustle and bustle that accompanies the departure of great ocean liners. The insistent, repetitive bellowing of the ship's horn amid great plumes of smoke, the silent and precise movements of the sailors, the shouts of passengers hauling their baggage down the metal stairs or through the passageways leading to the cabins. And then, suddenly, the dock began to move away, and the shadowy figures of family members and friends slowly disappeared. That was how he had begun the voyage that, after three days and three nights at sea, was to bring him to Marseilles.

7

Manuel had planned, virtuously, to devote this long flow of time to fruitful sessions of solitary meditation. He would lie for hours on his deck chair, facing the sea; he would watch the frothy, blue-tinged waves, driven by an imperceptible headwind; he would, of course, constantly have a book or two open on his lap: Flaubert, to be sure, but also Proust, perhaps (it would be a good time to try to finish it); finally, somewhere in a pocket, always at hand, there would be the small, brand new, black notebook, which would allow him to set down his thoughts as they came to him.

In reality, on the first evening, once he had settled himself on the upper deck in order to dream at his ease beneath the stars, he was surprised by the sudden and very noticeable cooling of the air; when, drenched and shivering, he decided to take refuge under his blankets, he was enraged to discover the constant rumble and the strange, vaguely nauseating odor that came from the engine room, near which was located, along with a few dozen others, his very rudimentary berth. The result was that he spent a miserable night. But by the following morning he had come to terms with these disappointments. He chose to pass these days insouciantly, as if he were on a pleasure cruise or heading off for an exotic vacation.

As it had on every crossing since Morocco had declared its independence, the Paquet company liner, the Djenné, was taking back to metropolitan France a load of officials and military men who had completed their tours of duty. A rather relaxed atmosphere. From morning until very late in the evening, the third-class bar – where he had quickly taken up residence along with some other young people of his age, the very ones occupying the berths next to his own – remained full: drinking, flirting, or playing card games, depending on the hour and the occasion, sufficed to make those present happy. A happiness in which he had been able to share quite casually, with the help of a frail, blonde girl from the Berry region nicknamed Bibiche, who had attracted him from his first morning on the boat.

At the end of this intermezzo, which was pleasant but ultimately not very conducive to meditation, there had been the uncomfortable train trip from Marseilles to Paris. A very different experience.

Because he had not reserved a seat (the travel agency that had booked the tickets had simply overlooked this detail), he had to stand in the aisle much of the way, in a car full of khaki uniforms and crew cuts, surrounded by soldiers smoking Gauloises and singing bawdy songs that chorused from one compartment to another. A whole day, under a sky for the most part leaden, through forests and fields, prairies, bare rocks, apparently deserted suburbs and countrysides. A whole day, during which he had nothing to eat but the tasteless ham sandwich he'd taken the precaution of buying when the train made a long stop at the station in Avignon. He had consoled himself by watching, as they passed by in their diversity, the landscapes of this France that he was happy finally to be seeing. Drawing on still-fresh memories from his school days, he attentively noted the name of each station as the train passed through it, deciphered from afar all the signs, identified the zones traversed, blithely mixing provinces, regions, *terroirs*, and *pays*. Dauphiné, Lyonnais, Bresse, Beaujolais, Bourgogne, Charolais, Morvan, Vivarais. So these were the concrete realities corresponding to the names that had up to then floated naked in his memory or else danced in his head like seductive bubbles of sound.

Finally, there was the arrival in Paris. The pale lights in the Gare de Lyon. The smell of damp railroad platforms. The shouts of group leaders. Family members greeting one another. The line to get a taxi. And it was at the end of a long, jolting ride in an ancient, rather wheezy Peugeot through overcrowded neighborhoods that he had been set down, haggard, with his two brand-new suitcases, at the foot of this ghostly building protected by iron gates.

In front of him, a low door, above it a barely legible number. The door seemed to him narrow, out of proportion with the place to which it was supposed to give entry. Dragging or pushing his bags one after the other along the sidewalk, he went up to this aperture, just barely avoiding a fresh dog turd next to it. Beneath a dim, yellowish light, a small, graying man in a wrinkled white coat too tight for him seemed to be drowsing behind a window in a sort of glass cage. The little man opened his little eyes, looked at Manuel without apparent surprise but also without friendliness, and did not even try to hide a little grin as he watched him struggle with his suitcases. With a weary gesture, he waved him in.

What happened next, Manuel did not have the heart to write down in his little black notebook, which thus remained, for the fourth consecutive day, stubbornly virgin. But for a long time he retained in the depths of his memory a veritable muddle of images. Images that varied in their fidelity and precision, as he discovered much later on, when he sought to bring them back to the surface: they rebelled, resisted his call, like the pages in a book one has not opened for ages that refuse to be separated because dampness and dust have gradually glued them together. Nonetheless, he succeeded in reconstituting, by means of a retrospective examination, the sequence of events.

This Arrival (with a capital A, of course), how would you characterize it, more than ten years later? Stations of the Cross would surely be excessive, and your friends who are believers would find it irreverent. An obstacle course, then? An initiatory itinerary? A little of both, but especially an assault course whose main points are grosso modo the following:

—you've hardly entered this new world before you find yourself wandering along dimly lit corridors where you meet, gliding along like shadows, a lot of other young people, many of whom seem (slight consolation!) even more lost than you are;

—successive stops in poorly ventilated offices, crowded with solemn wood furniture smelling vaguely of turpentine, and which, whatever your ignorance of styles and periods, seems to you to go back to at least the middle of the last century; there the formalities of registration are completed, at the end of which you are asked—very ceremoniously—to sign your name, carefully written in an impeccable English style, in a large book bound in black cloth;

—an ascension, with your two suitcases, toward the upper floors, where the laundry room is located; there, another wait, amid a strong odor of soap, steam, and hot irons, to deposit the required articles of clothing, each of which, marked with your initials and your number, is duly checked by a trio of smiling ladies (the first smiles you encounter); the youngest of the three gracefully exhibits, underneath a starched blouse that seems to have been molded right over her skin, very attractive curves (you did not yet know, on

that day, that the figure of the libidinous laundress has long been part of the erotico-poetic mythology of boarding schools);

— somnolence, for an indeterminate length of time, under the eyes of a little man in a little gray suit, with a black bow tie and a shrewish face (the inevitable monitor) in a study hall at first almost empty;

— the progressive invasion of the aforesaid study hall, whose door is soon ceaselessly opening and closing with a slight squeak that makes you jump every time, in order to let in new arrivals, more and more numerous, more and more noisy: most of them wear in their buttonholes the little metal owl that is, one of them tells you, clearly surprised by your ignorance, the symbol of the khâgne;[2]

— after a bell rings for a long time, immediately making every-one present get up and leave, in the greatest disorder, the first con-tact with the local food. The setting: a high-ceilinged, echoing hall, violently lit by buzzing neon lights, which serves as a refectory; the menu: vermicelli soup (light, light), a slice of roast beef (which you preferred not to try), small fried potatoes (you devoured them), green salad and stewed plums (edible, but they did not seem to you, alas, adequate to your hunger);

— to finish up, taking possession of a bed, chosen at random among at least fifty others, aligned in two serried ranks facing each other in a long rectangular dormitory with bare walls where you thought you immediately discerned, alas, whiffs of dampness (school architecture of our ancestors, who can express your holy, but so unhealthy, simplicity?).

It was the last day of September 1957. Manuel was eighteen years old. He had just become a resident student in *lettres supérieures* at the Lycée Louis-le-Grand.

This was certainly not the way he'd imagined things. He, who thought of Gavroche, Marius, Cosette, and Little Pierre[3] as child-hood friends, as close — and even closer, on some days — as his usual buddies, had very soon convinced himself that long, very long studies in the heart of the Latin Quarter would allow him to cor-rect the unfortunate destiny that had caused him to be born so far from the banks of the Seine. For months, in all his conversa-tions with Ariane and with Violetta, he had spoken of Paris as if it were an actual person, a full partner in everything he was going to undertake. Paris was everything for him: the ideal place, the home of daring, a unique mixture of the rarest qualities. There alone would be satisfied, for the time being, his most urgent desires, those he scarcely dared admit to himself; there, too, would be realized, in the longer term, his hopes for the future. The names of certain streets, of certain monuments, of certain institutions (and the Lycée Louis-le-Grand, formerly the Collège de Clermont, which luminaries such as Molière, Voltaire, and Hugo had attended, was obviously among these) were enough to set him dreaming. It seemed to him that the moment he set foot there he would be immediately swept away by their history, enriched by part of their glory.

Instead, there was . . . *that*, to which he refused to give a name.

The following period only gave him new causes for disappointment. On the first evenings, just before the moment when the monitor — in a hurry to get back to the wooden box that served as his loge — was about to begin turning out the lights, in accordance with the rule, Manuel couldn't bear to climb into his bed without another look, full of hope, at Paris. From the high windows that occupied one wall of the dormitory, he glimpsed — and even then he had to crane his neck a bit — a rather sad part of a rather narrow street, deserted at that late hour. It was lined with long gray buildings, in which faint yellowish lights pierced, here and there, the darkness. They were the buildings of the Sorbonne, which he was mortified not to have recognized, despite the fact that those façades had been so familiar to him for such a long time! In the short time he had been living in what was supposed to be the city of his dreams, it had become even more distant, even more inaccessible. He did not fail to reproach himself. To repeat to himself that all this was going to change, that he had to show that he was capable of determination, of patience. In vain.

In reality, he was not succeeding in acclimating himself, in the literal sense of the word. The humidity made him uncomfortable, bothered him, tormented him. It even seemed to him that it followed him around, everywhere, all the time, as if it were his personal enemy. The downpours that often came suddenly to ruin his walks in the Luxembourg Gardens, transforming them into races through the obstacle course of lanes cluttered with metal folding chairs, were already hard enough to bear. But what put him into a state close to rage, or despair, were the long – interminable – days of rain that followed each other without interruption, going on and on with the inept obstinacy of too-well-regulated machines.

He had, however, taken genuine pleasure in the discovery of autumn, and would have been ready to address to it, as had so many others, a few passionate odes, or even to make of it his special mental season. For it is a season he had hardly known in Morocco and that had fed his nostalgia ever since his childhood. *"Here,"* he had written one day, *"one never sees the sun grow pale, or the trees cover themselves with spots of red: what takes the place of autumn slips in belatedly, after months and months of an excessively long summer, and almost immediately it is over, without fog or fallen leaves."* Alas, in the Lycée's dark courtyard (later on, he learned that it was called "the bear pit"), autumn never had the poetic grace he thought he had a right to expect from it.

But if it had just been the humidity! There was also the loneliness. Manuel, who had been surrounded by people ever since he was a child, had arrived in Paris with an ample supply, accumulated without effort, of spontaneous friendliness, immediate cordiality. And he was prepared to lavish his friendliness and cordiality on others. On all those who were worthy of it, of course, and only on them, but he had no doubt that in a sanctuary like the one to which he had just been admitted, they would be legion. But his spontaneous friendliness and immediate cordiality had found no outlet. They remained unused, for weeks and weeks, like superfluous accessories he had brought along by mistake. They had therefore ended up going sour. And the ritual of hazing had hardly made things better. Confronted by the practical jokes and bullying that tradition requires the older students (pompously named "powers") to inflict on the new ones, a movement of solidarity had emerged. The new students whispered together in the halls, in the evenings after dinner, trying to decide on some form of collective resistance. He was ready to be the soul of this insurgency. But in the end the movement came to nothing.

13

In the days following the beginning of the school year, Manuel had thus seen most of his fellow students – who were at the same time his companions in the study hall, his neighbors in the dormitory, and his comrades in the refectory – form more or less closed groups, subgroups, clans, coteries, and cliques. A whole set of criteria – reflecting a society resting on age-old foundations and consisting of a network of strata too complex to be grasped by a boy who'd just arrived from another world – had determined the groupings. They took into account not only geographical origins but also membership in religious and political denominations, affinities in philosophy and in literary and artistic taste, as well as – and this seemed to Manuel the crowning touch – athletic proclivities. Within each of these groups were already developing – like so many barriers the elect threw up to protect themselves from the excluded – linguistic tics, coded jokes, and horrible little smiles of complicity. In this way he discovered the extreme fragmentation (Commies, Catholics, Protestants, movie-goers, readers of *Le Monde*, readers of *L'Equipe*)[4] of this community that he had imagined as devoting itself exclusively, in perfect agreement, to the cult of belles-lettres.

Surprised and dismayed, he was not even able to grasp the helping hands that were occasionally held out to him. Several of the older boys – real *bicas*,[5] rich with the experience they had acquired through their two successive failures to pass the exam, and who were preparing themselves for a third and final try ("you'll see, *bizut*,[6] it comes sooner you than you think!") – had shown him, along with the hazing, a very paternal friendliness whose sincerity he never suspected: among them was the rubicund, plump Melchior, who swore only by Blanchot,[7] and played, with a discreet pleasure, the respected role of ancient wise man; and then there was his antidote, Richard, pale and voluble, who displayed to everyone, in addition to his intransigent passion for Breton,[8] his strong Toulouse accent. These two had kindly explained to him, between two puffs on their pipes filled with Amsterdamer, a few little mysteries, such as the rules of the local slang, which he soon learned to use, or the origin of the nicknames given to most of the teachers.

Other older students, less distinctive than these two, and who no longer cared about keeping this worn-out folklore alive, had tried, with a perseverance and good will that impressed him, to draw him toward "the defense of the interests of the working class." He went along, because he considered the Left, on the whole, to be his natural family. But being little attracted by the charms of reading daily the gray columns of *L'Humanité*,[9] which seemed to constitute the core of their political activity, he had fairly quickly dropped out. There was no question, moreover, of trying to find in the other classes of preparatory students what he had not found in his own: second-year students, *pistons*,[10] and *colos*[11] liked to affect, at least intramurally, locker room manners and language (some of them didn't have to try very hard to do so), and in any case, with few exceptions, these good young people, kept constantly busy doing the countless exercises that rained down on them every day, had little interest in hanging out with literary types.

This unexpected solitude, to which he no longer had even the strength to oppose the old fund of Stoic ethics borrowed from the heroes of the passages he'd translated in his Latin classes, was not merely a disappointment. It was – no word sufficiently strong came to mind – an abuse of confidence, a pure and simple swindle. He was angry with himself for having let himself be trapped in this way. After all, he alone was responsible for his presence in this place. He alone had persuaded his parents of the absolute necessity, "for his future" (these words had been, in their eyes, the decisive argument), of spending some time in Paris. Whereas he could have, with their blessing, passed happy days doing a preparatory year of study, under the sun and the orange trees, in the sweet city of Rabat . . .

One of the rare moments in which his anger subsided occurred on Sunday mornings, when he devoted himself to writing letters. Manuel had made an effort to keep in touch with his little circle of friends back in Morocco, and from time to time he sent one or another of them a brief message. But all through these initial weeks, it was mainly to his sister that he wrote. Because he needed to, but also because it gave him pleasure. Ariane, scarcely a year older than he, had always been his closest friend, his confidant. This relationship had grown still stronger because of the affair he'd had with Violetta: Ariane had ardently followed its twists and turns, as if she'd felt that she herself was involved. They wrote to each other every week, just as they'd promised to do on the dock, before the Djenné sailed. She, faithful as always to her commitments, made it a point of honor to transmit to him, with precision and celerity, all the news, all the gossip and rumors that might amuse him: the couples who were getting together (*sweet Cleo with that clod Antoine, it's true, just imagine!*), the engagement of cousin Berthe to the handsome Serge, finally celebrated (*Practically privately, it's a real scandal, Aunt Zoé is still angry about it!*), cousin Pierre's marriage to his beautiful American (*Grandiose. No less than three orchestras. And a buffet ... Divine*), the Bernardots, the downstairs neighbors, have returned to France for good (*Soon, you'll see, we'll be the only ones left in the building!*). But she also questioned him. She wanted to know everything about life in Paris and the countless pleasures her "little brother" must be enjoying there. In general, wanting to do the right thing, he abstained from responding on these points, or else didn't address them directly.

Taking care that his disappointment appeared only in a light and oblique way, he sought at first (though it quickly became a tic) to fill out his letters with bad puns (he called the Sorbonne the "soeurbonne"),[12] hardly camouflaged literary allusions, and more or less comical anecdotes, all of this drawing on the cultural baggage they'd shared since childhood. He gave her a running account of the most picturesque moments in the life of the boarding school residents. The race to get lockers, which had begun on the first day: everyone had brought padlocks, some of them very sophisticated, and tried to appropriate as many as possible of the wooden lockers that lined the whole wall at the end of the study hall. The feverish crowd that formed every evening around the *bizuts* who served as errand boys (two were named each day, and all the *bizuts* had to do it in turn), when they returned from their round of visits to the creameries on the Rue Saint-Jacques, with their big bags overflowing with the delicacies they'd been sent to buy (including mountains of milk cartons), and that everyone was impatiently waiting to devour at the afternoon snack time. The shouts that for one reason or another, and most often for no reason at all, echoed from table to table in the refectory, taking the form of a genuine war of hymn-singing between the different classes of preparatory students: it was then that, to the tune of the "Trumpets of Aïda," suddenly went up, bellowed as loudly as possible by all the literary types for once unified against the common enemy, the "Vara," the *khâgne's* hymn, with its words in macaronic Latin (*Vara tibi Cagna vara celebrat gloriam . . .*). The more or less clandestine circulation of "dirty" books (the most prized were those of Baffo, Nerciat, and Crébillon fils) whose reading had to be continued, after the lights were put out, with the help of a flashlight slipped under the covers.

Regarding all the rest, he remained evasive. He didn't want to discourage her too much, his sweet Ariane: she would have so much liked to be with him in the city of cities, she who was waiting so feverishly for her turn to leave! So he didn't tell her everything. Not about the boredom. Not about the loneliness. Not about the disappointments he felt day after day. What good would it do to describe to her the spectacle, renewed every morning, of the vast dormitory with its fifty unmade beds? The lack of privacy in the tiny, old-fashioned showers, which were open – and for a short time at that – only two nights a week? The poverty of the afternoon snacks, which amounted to no more than a couple of slices of plain bread? The multiple vexations (short-sheeted beds, lockers broken open and pillaged, stolen mail) inflicted on a few wretches who had suddenly been transformed, no one knew why, into whipping boys? Little by little, however, he ended up feeling impelled to adopt a confessional tone, pouring out his feelings. Then he stopped giving reports on the present and started telling her about his hopes for the future. On that terrain, he could go on forever. He'd just discovered, in a letter of Kleist's read in one of the very first books he'd bought on the Quay Saint-Michel, the importance of having a "life-plan," and he'd immediately begun to draw one up, full of magnificent projects and comminatory injunctions addressed to himself.

Once the relatively calm moment of the mail delivery was over, he had to do the hardest thing – get through Sunday. Well before noon, the boarding school, which had been relieved the preceding day of everyone who could go home for the weekend, began to empty out: the hemorrhage reached its peak immediately after lunch. Many students couldn't even wait until the meal was over; they got up in great haste as soon as there appeared at the doors of the refectory, pushed by waiters in white smocks, the fragrant carts bearing the cheese plates. For all those who had a pretext for leaving, there was no question of going back to the prison of the study hall. They were only too proud to be able to escape from it, two or three at a time, in their Sunday clothes, and loudly proclaiming, with mysterious airs, that they were going "to town," and would probably not be back for dinner.

So like all the others, after taking off the long gray smock that constantly covered him, after having slipped plastic stays into the collar of his white nylon shirt, which he had himself washed the day before in his washbasin and hung up to dry on a hanger overnight, after having hastily straightened, using his little pocket mirror, the knot in his only silk tie (a gift from Ariane), he made it a point of honor to disappear.

To go where? Manuel didn't want to burden with his presence the cousins who had received him – very cordially, moreover – when he'd gone out for the very first time: passionate about bridge and chess, they lived in a closed circle in their vast, dark apartment on the Avenue Mozart. It was certainly not at their place that he was likely to make the kind of exciting encounters to which he aspired. And then he wanted to prove to himself that he was capable of initiative, of autonomy, damn it! So he chose to go to the movies, in the hope that perhaps, in this community of strangers that had come together for as long as the film lasted, a kindred soul, would some day . . . He rather liked the good-natured ritual of the showings in the little movie-houses of the Latin Quarter: lining up on the narrow sidewalk among couples clinging to each other and groups on a spree, the laughter and whispering of the spectators who had already found seats, the furtive brushing against other people in the shadows while the luminous ray of the usherette's flashlight led the way to one's seat.

The resources were numerous: by combining schedules, he could manage to see, in the area around the Rue Champollion, as many as three films before returning to the Lycée for dinner. It was assuredly a good way to complete his cinematic education, which was built around a few Hollywood stars whose images had haunted him ever since he was fifteen: Rita Hayworth, Ava Gardner, and Cyd Charisse. But despite the pleasure he took in changing to a different universe, in watching and rewatching *Les Visiteurs du soir, La Kermesse héroïque, Hôtel du Nord, La Grande Illusion*, or *Les Enfants du Paradis* (which had quickly become his favorites) he did not resort to this expedient without a certain regret or a guilty conscience: every one of the hours he spent confined in a dark movie theater, imbuing himself with flesh, desire, and sex, was an hour that he was stealing from the City of Light.

Therefore, whenever the weather seemed to permit it, he walked around the city. Every successive Sunday, he was burning with desire, of course, to explore Paris, as he had always promised himself he would. But he certainly did not want to lower himself so far as to consult a guidebook, to stand in line to get into monuments, to walk with a group up and down famous avenues and boulevards, in short, to be a tourist: the very word, despite its Stendhalian pedigree, horrified him. He had in view a far more profound kind of possession, at least in this very first phase of his intimate relationship with his beloved city. A possession that was to take the form of a frequent, repeated, indefatigable going back and forth at the heart of a few secret zones within the great body of the city, always the same ones, toward which he was, moreover, attracted by a very old fascination. It seemed to him that he could be satisfied only by the slow, meticulous impregnation that would result from proceeding in this way. Therefore he regularly strolled around the Luxembourg Gardens and the Pantheon, on the Boul'Mich and the Rue des Écoles, or else in the labyrinth of small, quiet streets over by the Odéon and Saint-Germain, where he tirelessly contemplated the display windows of merchants selling old books. He still hesitated to go further, and even when he was wandering along the quays, never crossed the Seine without distrust. Sometimes he stopped in front of a building whose animation suddenly broke the silence of the neighborhood. From a wide-open window on the second floor he would hear the echoes of a party: Louis Armstrong's trumpet, the voice of Sinatra, Piaf, or Trenet. He immediately imagined, on the other side of the drawn curtain, young couples of his own age carelessly laughing, dancing, embracing each other for all they were worth.

Someone in the dormitory told him one day about the Saint-Ouen flea market. He went there the first time out of curiosity, and already a sort of nostalgia: he expected to find in it the counterpart – amplified to the Parisian scale – of the souks in which he had loved to wander as a child, holding his mother by the hand. The place enchanted him. Soon the flea markets became one of the destinations of his Sunday walks. He could spend hours there. Avoiding the more upper-crust areas of the market in which there was an endless series of pretentious antique shops that looked like bourgeois living rooms, he plunged into the most crowded byways, paying no attention to the colorful fauna he met there, attracted on the contrary by the accumulation of heterogeneous objects that appeared at every step and whose names, uses, and provenance were unknown to him. "This jumble," he wrote in his black notebook, "*offers you, for the moment, the most faithful reflection of a society that you are clearly not succeeding in entering and whose mute remains you must be satisfied with contemplating in this way, right on the sidewalk.*"

Back at Saint-Michel, tired from having walked too much, he bought himself a newspaper – Le Monde if he could find a copy at the sole newsstand still open near the metro exit – and, in this perimeter where he was beginning to feel safe, he took a seat on the terrace of a café, almost always the same one. He chose a small, isolated table, as far as possible from the groups that were manhandling the flippers of the pinball machines, bumping them to get free games, and especially far from the jukebox, where, week after week, Dalida, the Platters, and Paul Anka competed in schmaltzy sentimentality. Without opening his newspaper, sitting in front of a glass of beer that he rarely got around to drinking (he didn't like the prolonged contact of his lips with the thick layer of foam that took up a good third of the glass), he remained there, following with his eyes the continual movement of passersby. Or rather of the female passersby. At least when they were young and pretty.

He had never imagined that there could be so many of them. They rose up from everywhere all at once, various in appearance, in size, in clothes, in skin. And for him the air was soon filled with their perfumes, their accents.

They were there, then, within reach, those "Parisian women," those incomparable creatures who knew so well how to combine daring with delicacy in matters of love. Not one of them seemed to notice him, or even to see him, amid all the customers sitting at tables (he could be very easily recognized: he was almost always the only one sitting there alone). But they didn't care about this male with pale skin who followed them with eager eyes. A few of them, whom he would gladly have chosen as the targets of his desire, dismayed him by committing before his eyes the most inexcusable of errors: they allowed themselves to be approached, courted, even caressed, without apparent repugnance, by slick, handsome hunks to whom this indulgence confirmed their flaunted status of "charmers" (the word horrified him as much as the thing). The others, for the most part, moved on, without slowing down, toward urgent and mysterious business he had no difficulty in imagining. Which brought his secret rage to a boil.

2

Violetta

Come now, don't feel too much pity, reader, and especially you, my delightful female reader with a tender heart (to whom these pages are particularly addressed), don't let yourself be impressed by the dark, and even—let's be frank—resolutely pessimistic tone of the chapter you've just finished (thanks, by the way, for having managed to read it through to the end).

This text, I'd have you know, was not written yesterday. It was written (and this is only too evident, eminent experts in matters literary have learnedly declared) in the middle of the 1960s. More than thirty years ago, then (were you even born then, you who are reading me?). In reproducing it here for your benefit, I have been unable, on several occasions, to keep from smiling. With the fond indulgence one reserves for one's youthful escapades. The fact is that I hardly recognize myself in this representation of my so unheroic hero. To be sure, like Proust himself, I didn't hesitate to give him my own first name, without going so far, as you will no doubt have noticed, as to give him a last name (a gap I really feel no need to fill). But as far as the rest is concerned, all the tragicomic trials of his first days in Paris, I admit that I exaggerated things quite a bit. Yes, to make this paper Manuel's disappointment and loneliness more dramatic, I considered myself obliged to strike the chord rather heavily. Once again, you mustn't, sensitive souls, take all that literally. The real Manuel, the only one who has to stand before the tribunal of history, was not, I give you my word, as unhappy as that! My very faithful friends from those ancient days, who don't resemble at all, thank God, the caricatures I gave of them here, can testify to that.

"Well, then, well, then," you will say (and I believe I even sense in your voice as a loyal reader, a trusting female reader, a shiver of indignation), "you have deceived us! Why did you toy with the sacrosanct truth in that way? Why did you make the picture so dark?"

"It's simple," I reply. "I did it for good reasons, for very good reasons. In other words, for lofty and worthy reasons of literary strategy!"

"What's that supposed to mean?"

"I was only applying, to the letter, the ideas I had, at that time, regarding what the first chapter of a novel should look like. For – as the use of the past tense and the third person singular sufficiently shows – I tried to adopt the form of the novel in order to tell this story. I have to tell you that I was planning a great, beautiful thing that might have been titled (I hesitated regarding the exact label) something like *Manuel in Love*, or else *Manuel's Apprenticeship, The Sufferings of Young Manuel*, or *The Confusions of Young Manuel*:[13] a genuine *Bildungsroman*, which would at the same time be an equally genuine "sentimental education." Goethe and Flaubert, to be sure, but revised and completed by Thomas Mann and a few others, no less!

Making my past into a novel seemed to me an absolute duty. Not, of course, in order to attempt, by the grace of writing, to transform into successes the failures and deceptions of my real life: this first sample shows clearly enough that that's not exactly the case! But rather because I feared I'd understand nothing of my real life if I didn't first create a parallel imaginary life, patiently elaborated, subtly constructed, following recipes that owed nothing to chance or arbitrariness.

I was, along with a handful of close friends – whom literary history has since spotted, classified, and honored according to their respective merits – an adherent of what was then called critical realism. A very fine doctrine, to be sure, which imposed on us a set of tasks as grandiose as they were vague: to give order to the world, to make it appear in its coherence, to reveal it in its necessity and in its movement . . . If I wanted to be capable of carrying out such a program, I couldn't limit myself, for the beginning of my *Bildungsroman*, to the rather neutral and, it has to be said, unimaginatively naturalistic descriptions my memories supplied. No true art without a clear separation from what one has experienced! A far more

23

profound truth was to be transmitted. I had therefore to make this initial episode as striking and intense as I could. In this particular case, I told myself, I had immediately to push the rupture between my hero and the world to its extreme point, since, it seemed to me, it was in this rupture that the very essence of the novelistic world was situated. And the better to demonstrate that whatever the hero's illusions on this point might be, such a rupture can hardly be overcome, I'd truly suffocated my Manuel in loneliness and frustration. I'd even brought him to feel bitterness, impotent rage – in fact, I'd brought him virtually to the threshold of despair. The implacable severity of youth!

But – I can now admit it to you, who've been kind enough to accompany me so far – this voluntary rigor, the result of a somewhat exaggerated seriousness (God, how serious one is at twenty-seven!), I was well aware that I couldn't decently imbue my whole future book with it. So I promised myself to bid it farewell, or rather to correct it, as soon as possible, in order to introduce the dose of distance and irony that, as everyone knows, the Bildungsroman must have. How did I expect to do this? By resorting to the simplest of procedures: the voice of a mocking narrator who would periodically seize, firmly and in the first person, the reins of the narrative, in order to criticize the means used, and to re-establish, after each novelistic deviation, the imprescriptible rights of truth. But I still hesitated, at the time, regarding the points in the narrative where it would be appropriate to make this sort of graft. Above all, I wanted to avoid any possibility of its looking like a simple artifice. I shall not conceal from you the fact that I continued to feel diffident on this point, and that I prefer, today as I did then, to postpone a solution to this technical problem and to resume the course of my confessions.

Well, then, I have to say that in reality, on each of these first October Sundays, I was much more surprised than embittered. My real letters, which Ariane took the precaution of preserving in their entirety, and which I consulted in order to confirm that my memory was not deceiving me, prove it beyond any doubt. This loneliness, so contrary to my idea of Paris, was so incompatible with the dignity of what I knew to be the City of Intelligence and Love that I couldn't seriously believe it would persist. It could only be a misunderstanding. No, the luminous capital of my dreams couldn't be this desert island! I was not so naïve as not to realize that Paris society was multiple, that it was difficult, even impossible, to perceive its true contours through the few samples that the fauna at Louis-le-Grand, the flea markets, or the cafés of the Latin Quarter set before my eyes. And then I still had the major, irrefutable argument: the model that Violetta had graciously given me. Had I not had with her a delightful foretaste of what must, in all logic, await me if I could be patient? Precious Violetta!

Tall and slender, with dark eyes that seemed to have been laid upon her broad, chalky white face, and long black hair done in the manner of Juliette Greco (as some people said, with clear disapproval), she was one of Ariane's friends, and all three of us were students in the last year of Lycée. She was already almost nineteen years old; I'd just turned seventeen. Our city (what good would it do to name it? These days it no longer matters to me whether it's recognized or not)[14] was at that time, at least so far as its so-called "new" or "European" part was concerned, no more than a rather sleepy little world that had effortlessly managed – a rare exploit! – to combine the ordinary defects of colonial societies with the manifold pettiness of provincial life. And so Violetta's arrival in our languishing Lycée was certain, despite the underlying anxiety that permeated all of Morocco in the month of November 1956, not to pass unnoticed. From every point of view, Violetta contrasted violently with our ordinary way of life, just as her Saint-Germain-des-Prés or existentialist hairstyle contrasted with the strict, Joan-of-Arc or sober English-style haircuts that were the rule in our world. Living alone with her mother, a still young and newly divorced English teacher, Violetta had a freedom of manner and speech that she owed to her Parisian origins (she'd been born near la Rue Mouffetard, close to the Contrescarpe, and was proud of it) as well as to a year spent in New York with her father, who lived over there. All this gave her a more than sulfurous reputation among other families. In short, proper young girls at the Lycée – most of them the daughters of military officers or civil officials, prisoners of the conformism that ruled their little caste – were discouraged from having anything to do with her. That did not bother Violetta at all, on the contrary: she liked to cultivate the image of the lone she-wolf. But it sharpened her caustic comments on the girls she condescendingly called *les poupettes* and their families: "A bunch of mediocre profiteers . . ." She'd gotten into the habit of working with Ariane, whom she had, with sovereign grace, immediately excluded from the infamous group of *les poupettes*. So she appeared quite regularly at our home on Thursdays or Sundays, in the late afternoon, happy to drink a glass of mint tea on our balcony: she took advantage of this to put the final touches on a philosophy or biology assignment, or to borrow a manual. That is what was to bring us together.

Both of us were marked, though to very different degrees, by our romantic readings, and our first common ground was our regret – our very great regret – that we lived in a climate so obviously ill-adapted to our ideals. Just try to be romantic in a country with such harsh light, without dusk and without fog, without windswept plains, without old, lonely, frozen gardens, without even a paving stone glistening after a storm! We quickly discovered that we had a common idol, Baudelaire. A Baudelaire whom we loved above all for his provocativeness. Instinctively, we'd sensed that there was a tormented sense of decency behind his satanic affectations, a wounded sensibility behind each of his would-be blasphemies. And that made him seem a brother to us. Begun on this note, our relations were soon, very naturally, to become deeper: almost daily, we exchanged poems, not very discreet private comments during the long recesses at school (which sometimes earned us scoldings from the zealous monitors), and whispered secrets on the telephone, sometimes accompanied, on my side, by little embarrassed laughs. We would no doubt have remained at that point, under the watchful and complicitous eyes of Ariane, if, in early May, Violetta had not gallantly decided to give matters a decisive push. In order to sweep away the doubt and indecision she sensed in me, she gave her *Blitzkrieg* (as she later called it) a romantic cachet she knew I couldn't resist. A few messages hand-written in pale green ink on large sheets of embossed paper redolent of a very discreet violet perfume – relics of the time she'd spent in an American school – slipped anonymously, on three successive nights, into my mailbox, did the trick. They consisted of verses taken from the pages of the *Fleurs du mal* most familiar to us. The first could be reduced to this not very ambivalent question:

Ces serments, ces parfums, ces baisers infinis
Renaîtront-ils d'un gouffre interdit à nos sondes?[15]

As for the two following messages, in which certain words were circled in red and situated on the page in such a way as to constitute genuine little poems within the original poems, they were even more explicit in their invitation. Everything went as she had wished. I immediately grasped – without any difficulty, it hardly need be said – the secret of the ostensible anonymity. When, brandishing my three sheets of paper, I tried to speak to her after school on Wednesday afternoon, she broke into a great, joyful laugh and, before I'd opened my mouth, she took the letters, put her hand in mine, and leaning over to my right eye ("it's my favorite," she'd admitted to me the preceding week, at close range, "but don't suppose that I don't like the other one, too"), kissed it very delicately.

"There, it's done," she added, without stopping her laughter, which immediately overtook me as well.

From that point on, things went very fast. Even faster than she herself had expected, so moved was I by the elegance of the way she proceeded, which seemed to me very worthy of a true *jeune-fille-de-Paris*. The very next day, we set up our amorous arrangement. In the middle of this spring, already as hot down there as the middle of summer, we became accustomed to get together, every time we had a free moment, in a nice little apartment rented by one of Violetta's girlfriends who'd gone to Corsica in order to prepare to move back there (at that time, the word "repatriation" was not yet in use) and had left Violetta with the key. I always arrived a good ten minutes after she did, for neither of us wanted to be seen together in that place. There followed long hours alone together. With the doors

27

locked, the shutters closed, and the curtains drawn despite the heat, we entered into a time that belonged only to us.

At first, we liked to sit down primly side by side on the big living-room sofa. No question of jumping on each other like animals whose only motive was simple desire. We wanted to preserve the intellectual tone of our relationship (which seemed to both of us indispensable for our dignity), and this dictated our behavior. I always began by asking her questions, more and more precise, about life in Paris, and especially about the mythical Latin Quarter where I was counting on being the following fall. After which, we exchanged our latest literary discoveries: for her, it was Laclos, Apollinaire, Colette, and for me, Cocteau, Malraux, Beckett. We sometimes even launched into discussions on subjects in which our competence – at least mine – was more than limited. One of the most memorable, which followed the reading in class of a few fragments of Sartre, had to do with the ways a woman could prevent her freedom from deteriorating into "facticity"; in another, we disagreed about the notions of *amour-goût* and *amour-passion*, whose pertinence Violetta vehemently denied. "For me," she said on this occasion with unaccustomed seriousness, "love is nothing other than my natural breathing."

These learned debates, which gave each of us a chance to speak more or less directly about ourselves, were conducted against a selective sonic background: the apartment had a monumental radio-phonograph and a very eclectic record collection. We set aside the many recordings of so-called Afro-Cuban music (it was currently fashionable), and gorged ourselves chiefly on Beethoven, the Beethoven of the symphonies and the quartets, who was first on our list of favorites – which seems to me today a very strange list, juxtaposing as it did Ravel and Rachmaninoff, Albinoni and Albeniz . . .

But we soon violated our excessively strict initial protocol, in order to devote ourselves to other jousts, other exchanges, other discoveries. Almost eliminating preliminaries, we replaced them, more and more often, with a slow and skilful session of undressing each other, punctuated by kisses, sighs, and shrieks of laughter. Very quickly, she had the idea of giving a fond nickname to each of the parts of our bodies, and even to our underwear. So that we never needed to use any item of the sexual lexicon unless it was explicitly mentioned in some poem one or the other of us was reading to the other (I recall that Verlaine provided us with various rather racy examples, which I dare not reproduce here). I liked to linger on her breasts: "Shaped precisely," she proudly murmured, "to be held in the palm of your hands, to become erect under your caresses." After which, sprawled naked on the sofa, or sometimes directly on the red woolen Rabat carpet (but there was no question, for example, of using the bed in the bedroom!) we applied ourselves, with constantly renewed ardor, to the practice of what she had herself called a very highly developed flirtation.

She had insisted on limiting, as early as our first rendezvous, the field of our common activities: despite her scorn for petit-bourgeois customs and her conviction that love has nothing to do with morals, she couldn't bring herself to break once and for all the taboo of virginity. A thorny and complex subject, on which our views diverged. I had, of course, tried to impose on Violetta, along with my opinions, my desires, and I certainly did not lack arguments to convince her of the inconsistency of her conduct. "You do too much or too little!" had become my refrain. She graciously agreed, without for that reason consenting to change her behavior. She even firmly assured me one day, between two of her most vigorous and most competent caresses, that no, it wasn't for her at all a question of morals, but something entirely different. Something I probably couldn't understand: a constraint she freely imposed on herself, and from which she drew an acute increase in pleasure. And she wrote out for me (in green ink, of course) a poem by Apollinaire entitled "Les neuf portes de ton corps,"[16] on which she urged me to meditate.

I understood that underneath there was, in her, a sort of blockage I couldn't penetrate, and that all my rhetoric would for the time being probably not be able to make her give in. So I had the wisdom to go around the obstacle and, caring only about pleasing my friend, let her manage things as she wished. Thus she led me – as our familiarity increased – and we were moving forward with real seven-league boots – on an intimate exploration of her long, slender, amazingly supple body. "A dancer's suppleness," she repeatedly called it. Everything was for us an instrument of pleasure: our fingers, our lips, our tongues, our ears, and even our teeth and toes (I say nothing, of course, about the rest: literature today provides, I think, enough about that). She knew how to direct me, by a few unforeseeable movements – sometimes lifting her spread legs very high, sometimes closing them on my head, or suddenly turning over on her stomach and rounding her thighs – toward unknown paths in the hollows of which my curiosity, always ready to be awakened, plunged without shame, wandering along them with an increasing delight: our trajectories were never completed without a pause, more or less brief, in the bathroom, where whatever desire might still remain in us exploded in a final burst of pleasure.

In this way the limit that had been set to our frolics was revealed to be, if not entirely theoretical, at least very elastic, and Violetta, with an unparalleled dexterity – on which I could only congratulate her – managed without any difficulty to make me forget it. This know-how, she was later to tell me, she had learned in a brief and stormy "friendship" with an Air Force captain (the members of this group enjoyed a favor among the ladies that was highly envied by the other local males) whose lessons on the subject of aerial pleasures had been extremely efficacious. But I have to say as well that she was capable, on certain inspired days – laughing, she would tell me then that she was "possessed" – of making all sorts of imaginative additions of her own. An inventive boldness that filled with admiration the ignorant young man that I was.

The game was pleasurable, then, even delicious. I had immediately gotten a taste for it, and missed no occasion to indulge in it, to the detriment of all other activities. It was interrupted at the same time as the school year, without complication and without pain. That was also part of our initial pact: "No sentimental nonsense, if possible. It's a promise, okay?" Violetta had said. As a kind of farewell ceremony, and also to celebrate properly our very recent success in passing the baccalaureate examination, she had suggested that we spend a real night together, a whole night: we promised each other that it would be an unforgettable night (I was sure she would finally make up her mind to use the bedroom). Ariane had been brought into the secret, and we could count on her complicity. But some strange scruple that rose up in me at the last minute caused the whole arrangement to collapse. The celebration couldn't take place in accord with the forms Violetta had prescribed. I had therefore insisted on offering her, in order to win her pardon, an exceptionally long tête-à-tête.

This turned out to be, despite the torrid heat that seemed to anesthetize the rest of the city, our fullest session: frequent visits to the bathroom, under the shower kept constantly running, had allowed us to retain, almost to the end, a remnant of coolness. But when toward midnight the moment to separate came, each of us thought we had to show that we were re-establishing our distance. So it was with a very dignified detachment – British composure, in the style of Major Thompson, was then in fashion – that we promised, joining for a last time our bruised lips and our still-damp hands, not to lose sight of each other. She did not yet know where she would be in the following months. Perhaps she would return to the United States. But sooner or later she would come back to Paris, our chosen homeland.

3

Intermediaries

So that was, dear readers, my affair with Violetta. You now understand why, relying on these memories on which I liked to lean in moments of doubt, I retained – far more than my hero did – an undiminished faith in the future. Which, like a good prince, before too long granted, as you will see, the reward for my confidence.

The episode I now take up has at least one peculiarity: it is the only one in this book that I have never discussed before. For that reason, it has for me the charm of improvisation. In the whole series of my earlier attempts to write a novel (those of the 1960s, which I've already mentioned, and also those that followed, which you will soon learn about if you continue reading), I was especially in a hurry to arrive at the incandescent heart of my story, the splendid irruption of Tamara, the glorious apparition of the Beloved. I had therefore passed directly, without any sort of transition, by a violent antithesis, from the most somber episode (the arrival, deliberately darkened) to the most luminous one. A classical figure of rhetoric, of course, but in this case an inappropriate maneuver, which I give up without regret. Not that I want, inversely, using an equally tired device, to retard artificially the entrance of my true heroine. There is nothing in that kind of hypocrisy (believe me, the word is not too strong) that pleases me. In reality, the itinerary that was to lead me to Tamara required, after the dark night of my first days in Paris, a passage through intermediaries. There were two of them, and the role of each was, as it should be, decisive.

First of all, there was Fabrice, the handsome Fabrice, suddenly thrust into my life about three weeks after the beginning of the school year. We were in Greek class, and I was presenting a page of Lysias's insipid *Plea for the Invalid*, which I'd not had time to prepare adequately. With difficulty, I'd translated and commented on the first two sentences when an unknown young man came into the classroom without knocking, carrying a pink note that he held out to the astonished professor as if it were alms. The exercise we were doing was immediately suspended, and all eyes turned toward the newcomer. Rather tall, with fine features, eyes of an intense blue, and thick, almost curly blond hair. For a reason that escapes me (he himself told me later that it had been a purely instinctive movement, such as he still sometimes has), it was next to me that he came to sit down. A happy impulse: like the movement called *clinamen* by the followers of Epicurus, it was to change the course of my existence for a long time.

As soon as he'd joined the class, Fabrice D'Hellouin quickly aroused everyone's interest, and not only because of the two capital letters and the apostrophe that adorned his last name. In a few days, the fascination exercised by his physique and the prestige he'd won by having recently published in *Les Temps Modernes* a brief and brilliant essay on seduction (Jankélévitch himself, people whispered, had recommended to Sartre that it be published!) made a him a star. Even the most sober professors – those on whose foreheads was already clearly perceptible the austere mask of the academic inspector-general – seemed to respond to his charm; some spoke of his charisma, which was described as Rimbaldian. Since my own culture had as yet only very slightly (actually, not at all) succumbed to the myth of Rimbaud, I'd sought my references elsewhere: the Stendhalian hero, of course, but also *le grand Meaulnes*,[17] or even, why not, James Dean.

What might have been only an accidental proximity was the starting point for an intense relationship. It had nothing in common with the traditional friendships between schoolboys and the more or less dubious exchanges on which they are sometimes built. Fabrice seemed to me to be distinguished by a constant requirement: that there be not a single ounce of mediocrity or complacency in his thought or behavior. This quite quickly won him my admiring friendship. In the phase of doubt I was going through, I had the impression that I'd found – at last! – a person who met my expectations. In a few weeks, he sent a breath of fresh air through my literary, philosophical, and political culture ("it's a real conversion you have to carry out, my friend, and at a triple gallop!"). Rimbaud and Lautréamont, Saint-John Perse, Schopenhauer and Nietzsche, among others, made deep incursions on it.

There is no need to say that in following this regimen I began to breathe more easily every day. All the more since, at the same time, as if by the wave of a magic wand, my relationships with a few other fellow resident students, Michel, Henri, Gustave, and Simon, had become more cordial. In the evening, when the after-dinner study period was over, when the monitor on duty relaxed the pressure, and then in the hallways or on the stairs leading to the dormitory, we spoke to each other without the stilted mistrust of the first days. Our curiosities and our interests overlapped and complemented each other. They wanted to know all about Morocco, which in fact they had a hard time imagining; for my part, I was in a hurry to become more familiar with the life each of them had earlier lived in his province, in his family, in his Lycée, in Bordeaux, in Grenoble, in Rouen, or in Troyes: for me, these were the fragments, so to speak, of my other possible lives, which I believed I could in this way recuperate. So everyone in our little group talked about himself: I remember the remarks made by Simon, who was so proud to reveal his family connection (and his perfect homonymy) with an admiral of the past century, after whom, he told us, a street over by the Plaine Monceau was named;[18] I also remember my dear friend Gustave (since deceased), who claimed with a straight face that his family name was in the Bible. Very quickly, too, there was talk in the Lycée of creating a newspaper, a sort of tribune. I was asked to participate in this project, which flattered me: I immediately promised to write a presentation of Ingmar Bergman.

Fabrice soon felt oppressed, and even suffocated, in the atmosphere of the Lycée (and yet, he was not even a resident student: how would it have been if . . . !). It took him less than three months to exhaust the charms of the first-year courses – which were rather austere, it has to be said, in those distant times when the weight of

Greek and Latin, far greater than it is at present, crushed more than one student.

The last Sunday before the Christmas vacation, the day after a party to which he had dragged me, without much success for me, in a "cellar" in the Rue de la Huchette, we had an interview the record of which I have carefully preserved for a long time.

14 December 57

Another lunch with F.

Dear, indispensable F.: I don't forget that he is the first of my friends — and up to now the only one — whose house I have entered since my arrival, almost three months ago, in this sweet country of France (Veil your face, o Hestia, noble protectress of hospitality! But no doubt you have no equivalent, generous goddess, among our rustic Gauls . . .).

His parents, whom I only glimpsed the last time (not very talkative, but very impressive, both of them, in the middle of their living room, immense and overloaded with sumptuously framed paintings: that's just the way I imagined these mythical beings, these Parisian grands bourgeois) are not there today. Neither is, moreover, the young maid (from Brittany, dixit F.) who'd served us coffee (no silly goose, that one, with her turned-up nose, her hairdo in the style of Brigitte Bardot, and her eyes as moist as her lips: I wonder if, with the handsome Fabrice . . . but let's keep to the subject).

So we get ready to eat alone in the kitchen, with its immaculate white tiles. Fabrice has poured a large can of cassoulet into a saucepan and stirs the contents gently with a long wooden spoon, wearing his perpetual dreamy look. That's when he suddenly tells me about his plans. He's had enough. He wants to leave everything behind. The Lycée, Paris, France, Europe. He's going to leave. For a few months. He doesn't yet know where he's going. Around the world, perhaps. Africa. Latin America. Arabia. The Indus valley. Japan. He's not sure. In those regions there's a whole world in which we will someday have to take a serious interest, right? There lies the future, he's sure of that. His parents? Reticent at first, that's normal. But finally in agreement with the project. Nice, huh? On one condition: that he resume his studies next fall, that he try, at least once, to get into the École normale. He promised. But it's only a promise, after all. He'll see, when the time comes.

His staccato speech — which he seems to be addressing to himself as much and perhaps more than to me — fills me with a mixture of envy and sadness.

Ah, he can allow himself this kind of fantasy. And with his parents' benediction! Such a folly would simply never have occurred to me. I've had more than my dose of exoticism . . . But I say nothing, of course, and limit myself to a bit of facile irony.

"I see, I see . . . Handsome Fabrice is impatient to cast off his moorings. Our ancient parapets seem malodorous to him, a bit rotten, perhaps. He needs the high seas . . . 'Ah! Let my keel break!' as that other guy says.[19] That's fine, even very fine. I can only approve, of course . . . But in the meantime, who's going to end up once again spending months all alone among a bunch of halfwits? I suppose I can always console myself by reciting every morning, backwards and forwards, the fable of the two pigeons[20] . . . That's what it's for, our cherished Greco-Christian and Judeo-Latin Kultur, isn't it?"

He smiles and does not answer. During the rest of the meal, we talk about entirely different subjects: Buñuel, Malraux, Bergman's latest film. It's only when I'm getting ready to leave that Fabrice seems to remember something. He strides down the long, dark hallway, lined with books, that leads to his bedroom. He comes back a moment later, carrying a large envelope, hastily torn open, with the sheets of a rather long handwritten letter sticking out of it.

"Here, before sailing away, as you put it, I'm going to give you something. I'm not sure how much it's worth, but at least you'll have to admit it's an unusual gift. Yes, you see, it's a letter. It came only yesterday. A letter from an admirer, as people say. I've received quite a few of them, you know, since the publication of my confounded essay. I haven't even opened them all. Why bother? It's never gotten me anywhere. Well, almost never. But this one's different. The chick's name is Sonia. Really exceptional qualities, from every point of view. Scout's honor! Even the handwriting, look at that. Enough to make a whole battalion of professional graphologists drool. As for the contents . . . You'll read, if you can make it out, what she says about my passage on the seducer's anxiety. It knocked me on my ass! Well, anyway, I'm formally handing the whole thing over to you. At least until I get back. It's your turn to play, pal! Tell the fair damsel whatever you want. That I've taken off to make a survey of the bordellos of Upper Egypt with my friend Maxime, or that I'm investigating the arms trade in Ethiopia for a magazine in the Ardennes . . . That'll amuse her, at least. If you handle things right, you'll make a girlfriend of her. That'll give you a little change from the girls at the*

Caveau de la Huchette, who are not really your type, so far as I've been able to see . . .

That's how I discovered the existence of Sonia, who was going to be, on the way to Tamara, the final intermediary.

It wasn't easy to decipher the letter: Sonia's handwriting, which lined up on the page in small, compact blocks like Chinese ideograms, puzzled me at first. In order to identify each word, I had to proceed methodically, making a series of hypotheses and approximations. An exercise all the more laborious because the text was dense and in no way resembled the more or less fawning banalities that the expression "a letter from an admirer" might suggest. It was a real discussion, more philosophical than literary, conducted in a rather sharp tone mixed with a great deal of humor: Fabrice's main arguments were dissected, and turned against him, with amazing exactitude.

When I'd finished my slow and arduous reading, I had only one desire: to see face to face, as soon as possible, the author of such a document. At first, I tried to convince myself that it was purely a matter of intellectual curiosity, that my reaction would have been exactly the same had the letter been signed with a masculine first name. But I soon had to acknowledge that this wasn't true. A large part of my excitement was clearly due to the sudden intrusion, in the form of this astonishing missive, of a woman into my life. For I did not doubt for a moment, despite the circumstances – unusual, to say the least – that had put into my hands a message not addressed to me, that Sonia had definitely come into my life.

I wrote to her (I've never been able to find, alas, the draft of my letter; however, I'm sure I didn't destroy it). She replied. We met.

She had agreed to meet me on the first Sunday in January, at the foot of the towers of Saint-Sulpice. I saw approaching, at precisely the appointed time, enveloped in what seemed to me, I don't know why, to be the long overcoat of a nineteenth-century conspirator, a rather petite girl with brown hair glistening with reddish highlights under the winter sun, and large, very bright eyes. I was as struck by her resolute air as by her extremely refined features: "aristocratic" was the first word that came to my mind, and it never left it again. But if all the boldness and questioning of youth were in her eyes, something adolescent still remained in the rest of her slight body. I knew right away that she was not The One.

We sat down in the only café that was open and ordered two big hot chocolates. The not very conventional, even rather fantastic nature of our coming together (I had repeated to her almost verbatim what Fabrice said when he gave me her letter), far from shocking her, made her laugh. Which immediately created a genuine complicity between us. She began to talk, in a voice that seemed to me a first a little high-pitched, but gradually softened. It was the first time she'd written to someone she didn't know. But since he was only a little older than she . . . She read a lot. Books, magazines, newspapers. She'd come across Fabrice's essay more or less by chance. She'd been struck right away by his irony, his radical pessimism. Astonishing in such a young guy, and one who seemed so talented. And especially on such a subject. She'd written her letter straight off, without re-reading it. Then she'd had a hard time making up her mind to send it. She wasn't sure her mother would have approved. Moreover, she had, as a precaution, given a name and address that were not exactly her own, but rather those of a relative.

In this way I learned that she was of Russian origin, that she'd lost her father, who was an archeologist and a Hellenist, when she was ten years old, and that she planned to study history or architecture (probably both, if possible). For the moment, she was studying for her baccalaureate examination in philosophy at the Lycée Molière. Then our chattering became more intense. It veered off into countless subjects, both silly and serious, and lasted for more than three hours, without a pause. Neither of us seemed to be making the least effort. The words came all by themselves, following naturally out of one another, and our replies surged up with an appropriateness that would have surprised us had we thought to observe ourselves during these moments. Fully satisfied with each other, both feeling we'd found an interlocutor at our own level, we decided to see each other again.

And that is how, from one encounter to another, through meandering dialogues punctuated by moments of silence, over a hot chocolate, which had become our ritual beverage, we gradually grew closer, without concealing from ourselves (far from it!) the depth of certain of our disagreements.

I liked the constant effervescence of her curiosity, a little less her self-assurance, her vehemence, which sometimes left me unable to reply. She, who admitted without shame that she had a "a very strong weakness for the decadents," who had been deluded by Barrès, enthusiastic about Huysmans, and translated with jubilation Rutilius Namatianus, did not hesitate to tease me, still more mercilessly than had Fabrice, about my literary tastes, which she was astonished to find so conventional, so academic. On the other hand, she delighted in the *Arabian Nights* side of my family legends, followed with interest the story, more or less embellished, of my childhood exploits in a distant land, and laughed at my descriptions – extremely fanciful – of life as a resident student. I had repeated for her the classification, by species and genre, of my fellow students that I'd begun for Ariane's edification: a sort of *Physiology of the Khâgneux*, with the whole obligatory pseudoscientific apparatus ("in the manner of Balzac, of course!" I felt it necessary to explain).

We sometimes walked together, at my request, through Paris. Then she took me, without a guidebook, without a map, without an itinerary, into in an inextricable maze of streets and squares, boulevards and avenues, that even the consultation of the big maps in the halls of the metro did little to help me elucidate.

This went on for several weeks. One Sunday evening, toward the middle of February, when we'd just finished a conversation in which, I know not why, we'd discussed at length Plato and his theory of recollection, Sonia told me she couldn't see me the following week. My disappointed and worried look amused her.

"Don't look like that, for heaven's sake! It's not the end of the world . . . Anyway, I have a very good excuse: just imagine, for once I'm spending Sunday with my family. Well, my close family, that is. Only women: my mother, my two aunts, and my sister. Well, at least the person I call my sister, Tamara."

This was the first time she'd said this name in my presence.

"Yes, I know, I haven't talked to you about her yet. The opportunity hadn't come up. Tamara is actually my cousin. My double cousin. Yes, right, double. Not only are our mothers sisters, but our fathers (may they rest in peace) were already cousins. Curious, isn't it? Since we were brought up together, we've always considered ourselves sisters. Twin sisters, even, since we were born only a few days apart."

"That's strange," I replied. "I also have a cousin of my own age, back in Morocco, and for a long time we considered ourselves twins. But we've long since lost touch with each other."

"Well, at least there's no chance of that with Tamara. We swore, whatever happened, never to separate."

I couldn't help admiring the convinced tone with which she'd said that.

Two weeks later, we met in front of Saint-Sulpice.

"You know, I told Tamara about you on Sunday."

"Oh?"

"And about our discussions, and our outings. That is, everything."

"And so?"

"Well, I can tell you, darling, it gave her a strong desire to meet you."

"That's a point in your favor, Tamara!" I immediately thought, and I felt a surge of gratitude to this cousin who deigned to show such a flattering curiosity about me.

Sonia no doubt perceived some sign of this feeling.

"You'll have no objection, I think, to her coming with us to the theater next Saturday. I'll try to get another ticket for the Chekhov, you know, the one we talked about the other day. Anyway, I've heard lots of good things about it since then."

Of course I had no objections. None at all. The idea of meeting this charming new girl – she was necessarily charming – whose existence had, for some reason, been concealed from me up to that point, could only captivate me. I felt, from that moment on, the very special kind of joy, full of curiosity and hope, that still today precedes or accompanies, for me, meeting any new woman.

4

Apparition

That evening, before leaving the study hall around six o'clock, Manuel was gripped by a sudden torment. He felt uncomfortable, now, in his navy blue, double-breasted suit, which made him look like he was going to his first communion. This old-fashioned get-up, which he'd never worn since arriving in Paris – was it really the one most appropriate for the occasion? But it was too late to change: the doors of the dormitory, which on Saturdays were opened just after the noonday meal, had long since closed. Nervously, he pulled up his socks, and using an old handkerchief, hurriedly put a bit of polish on his black shoes, which the long walks of the preceding weeks had worn and dulled. Then he knotted with more care than usual his chic silk tie, which he never wore without thinking affectionately of Ariane, and pulled once more on the points of the collar of his white nylon shirt, which had an annoying tendency to curl up. These precautions having somewhat calmed him, he went out of the Lycée without even looking at the concierge, and walked at a slow pace toward the Odéon to take the metro as far as Passy. He'd studied the itinerary the preceding day, and patiently waited to change lines at La Motte-Piquet-Grenelle.

Precisely at the appointed hour, he rang the doorbell of the apartment in the Rue Nicolo where, he had been told, Tamara lived with her mother and one of her aunts. It was Sonia who opened the door. She greeted him joyfully and made him come right in. Then she took a step backward to make way for her cousin, whom she introduced with a formality not habitual in her. And thus it was that, in the half-light of the entry hall, Tamara and Manuel found themselves face to face for the first time.

Never again had he encountered such a face. What struck him first of all was not the quiet obviousness of her beauty. Another trait, which went far beyond, seemed to him more remarkable: the mixture of purity, frankness, and good will that she radiated and that gave him, as soon as he set eyes on her, the certainty that she must be the bearer of something unique, something sacred. As if some beneficent spirit, finally hearing his cries of distress, had taken things in hand, Manuel suddenly found before him, alive and real, holding out to him in a gesture already full of a happy familiarity, her two fine, white hands, the very woman he had, for months, wanted to turn up and that he was no longer expecting to meet anywhere except in his imagination. She was the incarnation, so scrupulously precise that it made him dizzy, of the most constant, the most tenacious of his fantasies. This convergence, which seemed like a miracle, left him speechless.

Delighted and as if dazzled by the almost immaterial perfection of her features, by the harmony they composed, he did not initially think of paying more attention to their details, or of giving a name to each peculiarity of her physiognomy. It was only later on, when they had occasion to meet again, that, by successive brushstrokes, the portrait of Tamara was outlined for him: the ash-blond hair, falling to her shoulders and framing an oval face of perfect proportions; the big gray-blue eyes, soft and dreamy, which sometimes shone intensely; the very pale, transparent skin; the long, almost fragile neck, like a stem trying to find the sun. But he was immediately sensitive to the tone of her voice, which gave to each of the simple and cordial words she spoke that evening strange and persistent resonances. Nothing more was required for him to put all his confidence in her. "No, nothing other than happiness could ever come out of such a mouth for me," he decided. And he was certain that he finally understood why, and for whom, all those love songs, all those love poems, had been composed over the past three thousand years.

What happened, starting at that moment, was long to remain present in his memory, and even to take on, in the course of time, multiple and contradictory meanings.

They had not stayed long in the apartment. Leaving the entry hall, where Manuel thought he perceived a slight perfume of roses on the verge of fading, they had moved into a small living room that

seemed to him warm and inviting. Manuel was not inclined, gen-
erally speaking, to assess the arrangement of a room, the quality or
originality of a piece of furniture. One object, however, struck him
that evening: a beautiful silver samovar that seemed buried – as if
they had wanted to hide it from the eyes of the profane – in a dark
corner at the end of the room. He'd never seen one so refined. "Or
as feminine," he immediately added.

Afterward, they went to take the metro at Passy. Sonia had insisted
they get into the car at the head of the train, which was already full
of people. All three standing up, a little crowded together, they'd
begun a conversation on the supposed merits of the play they were
going to see. It was as they passed over the Bir-Hakeim Bridge that
a very slight incident occurred.

At this point, the train normally slows down (*probably in obedience
to the secret desire of those who would like to enjoy the view over the two banks
of the Seine a little longer,* he wrote a few months later). That evening,
the change in speed was so rapid and so abrupt that the whole car
was shaken by a kind of jolt. Tamara was thrown violently against
Manuel. Her breast brushed against him, and her half-closed lips
were, for a brief instant, so close to him he thought he could clearly
feel his new friend's warm breath on his neck. The jolt had forced
Tamara to catch hold of him, and her left hand had gripped Manuel's
right forearm. She removed it almost immediately. The rest of the
trip was spent in relative silence, broken by a few remarks by Sonia,
who commented, every time she could, on the names of the stations
they were passing through: she pointed out, by means of a remark
or an anecdote, the particularities of the streets, squares, or monuments on the surface above. Manuel, who was only half listening,
suddenly had the feeling that they were all traveling in time as well
as in space.

Another kind of silence reigned throughout the play. Manuel had
taken his seat between his two companions, on whom he cast, alternately, at regular intervals, brief glances. He tried not to focus, as
he would surely have done had he not restrained himself, on contemplating Tamara alone, who was still more beautiful against the
background of the blood-red velvet upholstery of the theater's seats,

its gilded loges, and its brilliant chandeliers. A great disorder had overcome his mind. Sometimes he was euphoric: so he was going to succeed, this time, in putting an end to this loneliness that had so poisoned him! He was soon going to have, without any doubt, a companion who corresponded exactly to his dreams! Sometimes he worried: what if she didn't want to have anything to do with him? If she were indifferent to him? The idea that a few minutes later the three of them would separate, that Tamara might not go out with them again, with him, for a long time, kept him from being able to take a serious interest in what was happening on the stage: around the schoolmaster Platonov, a strange little group was fussing – an Anna Petrovna, a Sofia Egorovna, a Vengerovitch, and others whose names he did not even remember. He was obsessed with only one thing: finding a way to ensure that Tamara would be there again the next time, that he would see her again without delay. Feverishly, he waited for the play to end so that he could take them out for a drink. But they were abruptly separated on leaving the theater. A heavy rain had begun falling. The two girls, panicked, jumped into a passing taxi, without having really said goodbye or arranging to meet again.

On the way back, in the metro, walking up the Rue Saint-Jacques, and even when he arrived at the foot of his bed, the image of the girl he had immediately named "The Beloved" did not leave Manuel. In the darkened dormitory, always a bit chilly late at night when the heat had been turned off for a long time, the regular breathing, accompanied by a few snores, of his sleeping fellow students made a reassuring background. Slowly, meticulously, he took off his soaked clothes, put on his pajamas, and slipped shivering between his sheets. And suddenly, without quite knowing when it might have begun, he noticed that a sort of murmuring, a scarcely audible humming was coming out of his mouth. Only three syllables, short like musical notes, and constantly repeated. He immediately stopped, fearing that some neighbor with a sharp ear, whom he had unfortunately awakened, might have heard him. Then he began again, but without making a sound this time. Clearly separating, in his head, the three syllables. Putting a strong tonic accent sometimes on the first, sometimes on the second. But especially rolling, in the Russian manner, the "r" of the last one.

He'd hardly succeeded in going to sleep when he awoke with a start. It was neither the sound of the wind, nor the cold, nor the various church bells in the neighborhood striking one after another, that had awakened him. No, it was a sensation he'd never before had: the painful sensation that he'd lost part of himself. Tamara . . . So he no longer needed to wait. Up to that evening, he'd had the impression that he was being deceived, deluded, abused, tricked. That he'd entertained a dream without relation to any reality. And now all at once reality had finally decided to conform to his desires. His dream now had a body, a face. Everything was going to take on meaning. Not only the hours of study, which would lose some of their austerity, even on those tough winter days when the lazy sun did not appear until midmorning. Not only the moments of leisure; he would now know to whom they should be devoted. Even the most trivial activities, the tedious task of shaving, waiting at the door of the overcrowded shower rooms, and standing daily in line in the washroom to make his evening ablutions, were going to be enlarged and, as it were, ennobled. Life was beautiful, finally.

5

The Tuileries

I can tell you this without fear, dear readers: there is not much to correct in this description taken directly from the novelistic sketches I made in the mid-1960s. To be sure, here again, as in the long chapter on my hero's initial disappointments, a cautious respect for what I took to be the laws of the genre (for example, the concern for a certain dramatization), added to my taste for the symbolic detail (what would a *Bildungsroman* be, I ask you, without a subtle sprinkling of symbolic details?), played a role. But on a few points only, which I thought myself authorized to invent and which it is neither useful nor necessary, I think, to point out here. Essentially – at least with regard to the reality of memory – I scarcely needed to exaggerate. How could I have dared alter that instant, which resembled no other in my life? Even today, when I think about it, I am still in its grip.

I've not forgotten, of course, the various explanations I later found for this event, and which I long repeated to myself as if they were formulas of exorcism: it's true that some people, one of whom I happen to be, have a gift for attracting to themselves the people they need (the appearance of Fabrice had strikingly confirmed that rule); it's true that Tamara turned up at just the right time to serve me as a landmark, a fixed point of reference, at a time when I didn't know what to do with my life; and it's true, finally, that a slow and very efficient incubation had taken place during this first winter in Paris, and I could hardly avoid, at the end of all those months of solitary disappointment, being ripe for a *coup de foudre*. None of that, however, seemed to me sufficient.

How I recovered from this dazzling experience, I no longer know. It's strange, but that's the way it is. I have only the memory of a few moments. For instance, the following day, in the half-empty

Sunday-morning study hall, I wrote, instead of the ritual letter to Ariane (whom I neglected for the first time), a sort of declaration, overflowing with lyricism, addressed to my new friend. I told her how I'd been bowled over by her mere apparition in the semidarkness, and tried (already!) to determine the reasons. I composed, in my small, cramped handwriting, sentences I intended to be moving or passionate: words increasingly swollen with grandiloquence thus allowed themselves to be set down one after the other with an unaccustomed docility. But after a page or two, I ran out of steam. Completely. What I'd written seemed to me misplaced, to say the least. So many good sentiments poured out on an almost unknown girl whom I had immediately erected into a muse, whereas I had exchanged with her, in a whole evening, hardly more than twenty words! I immediately tore my letter into tiny bits, fearing it might fall into the hands of indiscreet comrades. Afterward, I forced myself to wait for the message that Sonia usually sent to inform me of her intentions.

That week, the days seemed to me long. When Sonia's letter finally arrived, stupor and consternation . . . She limited herself to proposing, in two lines, that we meet on Sunday at the Passy metro station "for a little tour of the den of that old driveler Balzac." Nothing more. Not the slightest allusion to our last outing. Not the slightest excuse for the hasty departure on leaving the theater, when it had seemed to me that they were running away. Worst of all, nothing regarding Tamara. I felt this to be an affront. So then, Mademoiselle Tamara (and I insisted angrily on rolling that damned "r," like a rock rumbling in a torrential river) was no longer interested in me! Already! It was she, however, who had asked to meet me! She who had decided to come, with her siren's voice and looking like an angel gone astray among mortals, in order to insinuate herself between Sonia and me! And one meeting, just one, had been enough for her to judge me, to size me up, to reject me! What haste! I saw my dream of love evaporating before it had even begun to take form. I didn't feel I'd deserved that. But after this fit of rage, a little lucidity finally began to dawn. I had to recognize that, being entirely consumed (and as if dazzled) by the sudden happiness of loving, I hadn't done much to make myself loveable.

On Sunday, with Sonia, I made great efforts to conceal my bitterness. After making our visit to Balzac's home, which took place almost in silence and was much shorter than planned, we went to the Ranelagh movie theater, which was nearby, an old theater whose woodwork Sonia wanted to show me. It was showing *The Lady from Shanghai*. We went in without hesitating. Orson Welles was one of Fabrice's idols ("An overwhelming genius, old man. Almost monstrous. In the line of Renoir and Stroheim . . ."), and it was high time to enroll him in my pantheon. But while the mirrors were being endlessly shattered on the screen, I was figuring out a clear line of conduct. Do everything possible to avoid returning to the loneliness of October. Therefore, above all avoid running the risk of annoying, by some tactlessness, the girl who was for the time being my first and only true friend, Sonia. I knew I could count on her fidelity. As for Tamara, before making an effort to find her, take time to think. A week, let's say.

A week even more tormented than the preceding one. Sonia's letter did not arrive until Friday afternoon. Very short. But containing, in a luminous postscript, the big news: Sunday at three o'clock, for a walk in the Tuileries gardens ("let's hope the weather won't be too bad"), there would be three of us! I had less than two days to prepare myself for the event.

What I could expect from this further meeting, I was not quite sure. The long days during which I feared I'd never see Tamara again had made her, despite a few explosions of anger, even more dear to me. Her return, obtained without my having had to carry out any of the absurd plans I'd drawn up (such as climbing the wall in order to go, several nights in succession, to wait in front of her apartment building in the hope of seeing her come out), filled me with gratitude. In addition, it opened avenues that my imagination, which was always ready to get excited, could explore. Who knew what Tamara had in mind? By delaying our second meeting in this way, perhaps she'd been seeking, by an innocent ruse, to make the pleasure of seeing each other again still more intense? I indulged in the craziest hopes: seeing her immediately throw herself into my arms, her eyes shining, hearing her murmur that she had understood me; reading on her lips, very near my own, the litany of "yes"s she'd prepared to reply to the overflowing of my mute questions. Yes, she'd felt the same jolt I had when we first saw each other, yes, she'd suffered as much as I had during those long days, yes, I was the one she'd been hoping for, waiting for, wanted, yes, we were now bound to one another forever, yes, yes, yes, a thousand times yes . . . But I was well aware that nothing like that would happen. It would have been too wonderful! I was prepared to come down, to be satisfied with a great deal less. A sign, a single sign, no matter how slender and discreet, provided that it allowed me to believe that she accepted the birth, between us, of "something." "Something" I wanted, for the moment, to call only understanding, complicity.

I had to wait, that day, torn between hope and anxiety, until the very end of our walk in the deserted Tuileries garden. It was after six. It looked like rain, the evening fog was beginning to come up. Tamara remained silent, with an attentive, concentrated air I didn't know how to interpret. Nonetheless, she made an effort to smile every time our eyes met. "What does she need to think so much about?" I kept saying to myself. Sonia, as if she'd felt how tense I was – though I was trying, of course, not to let anything show – had begun to talk: she'd obviously consulted, the preceding day, some old, learned study on the history of the Tuileries during the Revolution. Her erudition made my head spin. Not a single detail was lacking: the Salle du Manège where Louis XVI sought refuge during the day of 10 August, the round pond from which the great cortege left on the day of the festival of the Supreme Being, and many others. The monosyllables I uttered in response to the questions she asked me in order to confirm this or that point (precisely this period being part of the history program I was studying) had been sufficient to keep up a semblance of conversation.

It was only at the moment of saying goodbye, on the platform of the Concorde metro station, that I received my reward. Tamara suddenly recovered her good humor. She spoke last. In a calm voice, but one in which I thought I discerned some sort of vibrations, she declared that she was henceforth going to take part regularly in our outings. If we didn't mind, she added, smiling, and looking me in the eyes with, it seemed to me, a slight insistence. She had just signed with me the pact that I was waiting for. I would have liked to throw my arms around her.

When they'd left, making little signs with their fingers through the windows of the subway car, I had to remain on the platform a few minutes. Seated. Without even hearing the bum who, right next to me, was snoring on the wooden bench.

Then, going back up into the open air, I decided, despite the rain, to return to the Lycée on foot.

6

Tranquil Happiness

The tacit agreement with Tamara in the Tuileries allowed Manuel to enter a period of true happiness, the first he'd known. His fears vanished. He could envisage the coming days with serenity: he was now assured of being able to go out with two persons he loved intensely, even if the love he bore them was certainly not of the same nature.

When he thought back on his morose wanderings the preceding fall, on that long torment that looked like it would never end, the change seemed to him miraculous. He had finally landed on the shores of the Promised Land, and he was ready to thank his lucky star, destiny, Providence, or – under whatever name it might be given – the beneficent power that had brought him to such a good harbor. Nonetheless, the very well-behaved threesome he formed with his two companions did not exactly favor, in any way, explosions of amorous madness, the voluptuous overflows he had not stopped dreaming about ever since his first contact with Tamara. But he decided that the most judicious thing to do was to accept it. He even made of it, sometimes, a reason for being proud. Gustave and Simon had seen him, one Saturday night, after coming out of the Comédie-Française, drinking and laughing with Sonia and Tamara, the two of them in particularly high spirits, in the back room of a brasserie near the Palais-Royal; the next day, they did not hesitate to tell him, their voices loaded with insinuations, that they found his situation very enviable (this was said, of course, in the half-salacious, half-cynical tone always adopted by the resident students when talking about such things); he swelled with pride, not feeling any need to disillusion them regarding the nature of his relationship with his two girlfriends.

During this time, things retained, at least on the surface, a perfectly innocent character, Sonia's presence serving as an excuse for Manuel's blissful indolence. Curious and dynamic, Sonia made every effort not to miss anything important: she studied the theater posters, consulted the programs in *La Semaine de Paris*, read indiscriminately the so-called cultural weeklies (*Les Nouvelles Littéraires*, *Arts*, *Les Lettres Françaises*), taking pleasure in pointing out that their supposed political differences did not prevent some surprising critical agreements. Tamara and Manuel let her plan things, going along with her suggestions, applauding her injunctions. As if it were enough for them to be able to think of nothing but the joy of being together, of the pleasure of exchanging, every time they could do so without being seen by their effervescent guide, sometimes complicit smiles, but most often dreamy looks.

It was at the Easter vacation that the situation changed. Sonia began to be less assiduous: business whose nature she did not feel the need to explain – and regarding which Manuel did not feel the need to inquire, either – prevented her, she said, from accompanying them, leaving Manuel and Tamara alone together more and more often. But although it was periodically deprived of one of its members, the original threesome had not for all that been transformed into a couple. The shadow of the absent member, vigilant and vaguely disapproving, still hovered over their meetings.

There was, of course, behind the protestations of "deep friendship" or "warm affection" that served as farewells in the weekly missives that Tamara and Manuel now exchanged, an attraction, or rather an élan, that was as strong as it was sincere. But this élan didn't feel any need to declare itself: it seemed satisfied with the nourishment it was given, chiefly in the form of "outings." These outings had become so important for Manuel, who was finally discovering the pleasure of repeating in writing the intense moments of his new life (the very ones that once stubbornly refused to allow themselves to be transcribed), devoted to them, one Sunday evening, a long note – into which he did not hesitate to insert certain fragments taken from his very first letters to Ariane.

April 1958

"Going out with Tamara": that has become your most regular activity, the

one around which everything is structured. Your rendezvous have acquired the rank of rituals, which require your efforts to arrange in advance. You especially like the last-minute consultations that, since Sonia's defection, you have to have in order to draw up the program of your delights.

Some Friday evenings, just after showering and before going down to the refectory, you're proud to see coming toward you, tipsy and unsteady as usual, Eugène (called Hugène, called Gégène, called The Gross),[21] the old messenger whose entry into the study hall is, by tradition, the occasion for a loud uproar (nothing like it, be it said in passing, for creating an air of bacchanalia in the middle of an ordinary classroom). Mumbling your name, which, while pretending to be making a great effort, he never succeeds in pronouncing correctly all the way to the end, he makes his way toward you and deposits on your table, still with the same clownish compunction, the object of which he is the not very diligent bearer: an urgent message, in the form of a very light, wrinkled envelope, covered with a long series of postage stamps which are themselves covered with an equally long series of postmarks (five or six at least, sometimes more). At first sight, the latter seem to have been put on any old way, one after the other, by some careless postal employee. But you prefer to see, behind this apparent negligence, the zeal of an official aware of the urgency of the information transmitted and legitimately concerned to reduce the administrative protocol preliminary to the forwarding of the precious envelope. For this envelope is nothing other than a pneumatique,[22] the one by which Tamara, upon reflection, proposes that you rectify certain of your choices. You must reply right away by giving her a ring, the sole occasion you have to call her.

Phoning her is not always easy to do. There is, for the whole Lycée, only one telephone that students can use. It is located in the entryway, behind the concierge's loge. It is not a real telephone booth, but rather, installed at head height on the wall, a curious metal contraption, dirty green in color, that looks more like a helmet with huge wings, under which one has to take shelter in order to try to preserve, at least theoretically, the secrecy of one's conversations. Before getting to it, one has to get the obligatory token. One can, in theory, buy them on the spot from the concierge, but not rarely (in fact, frequently) the latter, who has little interest in predicting the fluctuations of telephonic demand among the residents, runs out of tokens, especially toward the end of the week. As a result, those with foresight — of whom you are one, since you have girlfriends to call — always keep, carefully stored in a small tin box they try to conceal from the covetousness of their hapless fellows, a few extra tokens. After which, one has a long wait in line for one's turn, in the drafty entryway.

As the dinner hour approaches, the line gets more and more anarchical. Keeping one's place requires a twofold effort, intellectual as well as physical. One must not let oneself be pushed around too much, of course, but at the same time one has to discourage — by means of comic invectives (the model is to be found in Captain Haddock's barrages of insults),[23] more effectual than the mere croaking in use elsewhere — the repeated attacks of a few inveterate line-jumpers. All this while putting up with the unbearable prattle of those who succeed each other under the helmet. When your turn finally arrives, you're obviously no longer in any shape to have a romantic conversation with Tamara. You're happy, however, to be able to hear, right in the middle of the Lycée, her voice, whose sweetness even the telephone has not altered.

As in Sonia's time, the range of your possibilities is fairly open: a play or a concert on Saturday evening; a museum, an exhibition, or a simple walk on Sunday afternoon. You were happy to get to know and discuss with her some of the films you hear talked about at school. Quite recently, it was The Bridge on the River Kwai; you did not hesitate to draw a parallel between Colonel Nicholson and the Boïeldieu of your cherished Grande Illusion. But it is the theater, in its most classic, and even most hieratic, form, that is by far your favorite.

This common taste comes to you from your childhoods. You've learned that like you, Tamara devoured early on all the novels about the lives of traveling players. That she spent, as you did, whole Sundays declaiming, before a mirror, long speeches learned by heart in her Petits Classiques Larousse. You loved the grandiloquence of this language, but you loved especially (as you have just realized) seeing performed on the stage all those actions that reality hardly ever allows us to see, much less to carry out. One of your greatest moments of enthusiasm you owe to a performance of Medea in Greek (only the masks were lacking!), which transported you into a world in accord with your dreams: the pleasure of letting yourself be rocked by the language of Euripides, made alive and musical again, so different from the aseptic Greek of your translation exercises; the enchantment of watching the move-

54

ments of the group of girls that composed the chorus, and who seemed (not by accident!) to have descended from the Panathenaic frieze.

Thus you nourish — and you are not the only ones — a special fondness for the TNP.[24] You are careful not to miss any of its productions — Brecht as well as Chekhov or Pirandello — at Chaillot. You are taken by everything about this place, which you are not far from considering a temple: the ceremonial aspect of the performances, the large number of theatergoers who, disciplined and good-humored, take over the great stairways, and even the music played over the loudspeakers at the ends of the intermissions. You sometimes regret, however, that there is not, as there was in Athens on the occasion of these great gatherings, a comedy after the tragedies.

Your Saturday outings are often preceded by a goûter dinatoire: Tamara was the first person you heard use this expression, and you thought she'd invented it herself to designate the light meal that she's preparing and that you find already laid out on the little table in the living room when you arrive. The Russian tonality that is largely predominant in the choice of dishes gives you simultaneously the pleasures of exoticism and those of familiarity.

You have rediscovered, with emotion, the forgotten use of the samovar; together, you dip out of it, as you did on holidays in your childhood, the water for the tea: but the delicate device, artistically worked, that hums discreetly in the background of Tamara's living room has neither the imposing size nor the brilliant coppery glints of the one that sat enthroned, its high cylindrical chimney topped by a goblet in the form of a skull cap, in your parents' dining room. You had no difficulty in accustoming your palate to a whole series of unknown dishes: there are smoked eels, marinated sprats and herrings, sometimes also pâté de foie, blinis, or succulent meat-filled pastries.

Sometimes the schedule does not allow a goûter dinatoire; those are the times to take Tamara to a restaurant after the show. Up to this point, you've had, so far as restaurants go, no experience other than that of the self-service places on the Boul'Mich, La Source, or Capoulade, and their mediocre meals on a tray. Fortunately, you've found, during a walk on the Champs-Elysées, a brasserie frequented by quiet young couples. Hidden in a lateral wing of the Lido passageway, it doesn't seem to you too unworthy of your friend, while at the same time being compatible with your resources. You're proud to be able to go in there from time to time with her, choose a table for two far from the bar, study the mysteries of the menu, which lists a series of dishes with grandiose names, request, in a confident voice, explanations from the waitress in her little white cap (it's always the same one, who envelops you, each time you come in, in a broad, friendly smile), and finally order, for Tamara and yourself, meals that contrast with what you ordinarily eat.

In this domain, you take care to harmonize your desires, to combine them as best you can. This allows you to double the pleasure you take in these gourmet expeditions. For instance, the last time you went to this restaurant, last night, you initiated each other—sometimes by giving samples to one another, sometimes by boldly taking bits off one another's plates—to the complementary delights of the two specialties of the house. You found heavenly the taste of the first bite of her Norwegian omelet she gave you, as if to start things off, and you couldn't help sighing with pleasure when she carried to her mouth, cautiously, because it was still hot, the big piece of flambéed banana you gave her, on the end of your fork, in exchange.

This period was also the one in which Manuel was finally able to penetrate the arcane secrets of Paris, of the Paris that had been the indulgent companion of his feelings of sadness in the autumn, but which he had always known, was absolutely sure, would sooner or later be associated with his joys. His explorations, systematic and methodical, were henceforth pursued in a Paris that had finally yielded to spring.

He had never, up to that point, had occasion to notice a city's beauty. Nothing had prepared him for this. The few cities in Morocco he'd been able to visit with his family had awakened, with the exception of the old part of Fez, only a few responsive echoes, and still less aesthetic emotion. At that time, for him, beauty could be found only elsewhere, far away, on the other side of that sea one had to cross, at any price, if one wanted to gain access to the real world.

With Tamara, he discovered a somewhat more ordered Paris: the expressions "east" and "west," "right bank" and "left bank" took on meaning. He was able to name almost all the bridges, at least those in the center of the city. He saw emerging the configuration of a few quarters other than his sempiternal Boul'Mich: in succession, the Halles, the Marais, Montparnasse, the Bastille. He perceived vicinal relationships between some of these quarters (from Saint-Germain-des-Prés to Montparnasse via the Rue de Rennes). Even the mystery of the bus system, which had at first seemed to him impenetrable, was gradually clarified: he began to associate certain numbers with certain itineraries. It seemed to him that each time he'd progressed a little further, and he felt more and more at ease, even in places where up to then he'd felt himself to be only in transit. It's true that, in order not to cut too poor a figure in front of Tamara, he had, for his part, begun to study the city; he'd bought on the quays two or three books that helped him acquire some knowledge of old Paris. But in fact, it was through her alone that Paris was gradually returned to him. A less phantasmagoric Paris than the one that he'd constructed through his dreams and his readings.

What never ceased to delight him was the familiar nature of the relationship between Tamara and her city – the exact image of the intimacy he himself was so eager to achieve – and, still more perhaps, her aptitude for divining, wherever she was, what they had called "the underside of the painting." She set the day and the time when it would be good to go together to sit on a still-warm bench in the courtyard of the Palais Royal, to stroll under the lime trees in the Place des Vosges, moving away a bit from the trees the better to smell their fragrance in all its intensity, to wander about among cartons of old books, with an unreal light filtered by high stained-glass windows falling on them, in the labyrinth of the covered passageways of the Bibliothèque Nationale, to steal a quick glance at certain very secluded gardens in the Rue du Bac, which could scarcely be seen from the outside through grill-work and iron bars, or to see the sun set near the Arc de Triomphe and the streetlights come on all at once along the Champs-Elysées. She also knew how to call a halt in front of a townhouse in the Marais or the Île Saint-Louis in order to point out to him (with simple gesture of her right hand, her raised index finger seeming to caress the building from a distance) the harmony of its façade, the elegance of its door, or, late on certain afternoons, to climb to the highest step on a Montmartre stairway, in order to have him observe the change in the light.

Every place he discovered with her was now connected with a word, a look, a gesture. The first time they'd crossed the Pont-Neuf together, they were very early for the matinee at the Comédie Française to which they were going; like two other young couples before them, they took the time to stop, right at the middle of the bridge, to watch the water flow underneath them; Manuel had put his right arm around Tamara. Ever since, when the weather was favorable, almost every bridge they went over was the occasion for adopting a similar position: then nothing seemed to separate them any longer, and they came out of their silent reverie only when they were approached by one of those itinerant photographers who are found wherever people walk.

Another time – it was at the metro exit on the Place Saint-Michel – they had stopped to listen to a young violinist who was playing outside, proud to exhibit his virtuosity at the foot of the fountain, from which there silently seeped, behind him, a slender stream of water. A small crowd had formed. In the front row of the admirers, hand in hand, the two of them attentively watched the rapid sawing back-and-forth of the bow, which the musician, concentrating, manipulated with an expert alternation of vigor and gentleness. But Manuel quickly noticed (for he couldn't help, under any circumstances, secretly looking at her) that Tamara, who usually abandoned herself completely to the music, holding her breath as if she feared she might miss the slightest note, did not hesitate on that day to stop listening for a moment and briefly turn her shining eyes on him, to be sure he was really sharing with her this instant of pleasure.

Thanks to a few moments of that kind, he went about the city as if passing through a network of intimate signs, and the map of Paris began to seem wholly like a *carte du Tendre*.[25]

He felt that they were in this way inventing, step by step, all the rites that would later become so many symbols of their progress toward love. That they were forging the elements of what would not fail to be, very soon, their common past. *"Our common past,"* he noted one day, *"was there long before we met! The same situation of pampered children, same tastes. But above all, parallel dreams."*

Now that Sonia had gone away (definitively, it seemed to him), he thought it was to him that Tamara was close, that it was him alone of whom she could rightly say that she was the twin. And he took pleasure in believing that they were soon going to realize – as in the passage from the *Symposium* he had not feared to comment on in class with an enthusiasm that surprised his classmates – the old utopia of one being in two persons.

7

The Extent of the Damage

Concerning the period dealt with in this new chapter of the projected novel, I have said from the outset that it was, for Manuel, a phase of true happiness. And it is with an almost equal happiness that I have copied out and inserted here those old pages. But you, persevering reader – perhaps you have taken them in only with a certain distrust. Alerted by my earlier admissions, you are probably wondering whether they are credible, whether they provide an exact reflection of reality, in a word, whether the apprentice novelist of the 1960s was able to forego his habitual manipulations.

Once again, the answer will be yes. With the exception of certain details, of course. For our incorrigible demiurge, with whose methods you are becoming familiar, was not able to avoid exaggerating here and there. If only to accentuate still further, for the benefit of somewhat myopic readers (there are more of them, alas! than one thinks), the contrast with opening chapters, which are so pessimistic. But let's grant him at least this much, that he kept within limits that were almost reasonable for the period. Above all, he did not want to see his novel suddenly go from black to rose-colored! And it is this same concern that led him to insert, in various selected places, under cover of realism, a few invented details, which may have only a symbolic value, and which he left it to each reader to perceive.

What I have to add at present is that this succession of tranquil moments of happiness did not deprive me of all discernment. I managed not to deceive myself regarding the fragility and ambiguity of my situation. You demand proof? Well, consider how I analyzed things on the day after one of our most significant outings (an overwhelming Piaf recital at the Olympia):

April 1958 (a note begun during D.'s class on Descartes's Treatise on the Passions. You could call it "The Actual State of Affairs").

All right, then! One of these days you're going to have to stop being such a dupe. The dupe of the detours and escape hatches your cowardice invents. You're going to have to admit it, at least to yourself. Yes, you love her, you desire her, you want her . . . Call it what you will, it's not words that are lacking, but admit that you think of nothing but that! To the point of having slipped into your last philosophy class paper (on a subject made to measure for you: "What is a true feeling?") a whole page on the caress (with supporting quotations from Montaigne and Spinoza!), which got you a big question mark in red ink from good old D., who gave you an odd look when he handed back your paper a little while ago.

The evidence is there, it's obvious, and even downright ridiculous. You've seen the metamorphoses taking place in yourself, one after the other, you've seen the attitudes obligatory in such a situation repeating themselves. No symptom is lacking, not even — and this is a great novelty in an inveterate sleeper like you — loss of sleep. So almost everything you happen to see, read, feel, or think in the universe of the boarding school, which is, after all, quite closed, brings you back, in the most unexpected ways, to her. When you're taking a shower, soaping with both hands and redoubled vigor, some part or other of your body, or when you're trying, without success, to control the force of the showerhead that's spraying you. And even in the refectory, when you dreamily stir your bowl of café au lait in the morning, or when you nervously manipulate your fork and knife at dinner. As if it were around her alone that the unity of your self could be constituted. So now admit it: there is no longer any part of your flesh, any atom of your mind that is not filled with her image, her perfume. Your obsession is capable of incorporating everything, of converting everything into an accessory. And, since for you everything is already rooted in words, you're beginning to understand, from the inside, what expressions like "to be beside oneself" or "no longer belong to oneself" signify.

Look hard at the oddness of some of your reactions: how much it seems to you that every time you leave Tamara, her smell, in which you think you discern, implausibly, something of the figs, almonds, and apricots of your childhood (how could one better define it?), persists in you for a long time. It follows you in the crowded metro cars on Sunday evenings, it walks with you

through the corridors of the Lycée, it makes you forget the unpleasant ex-
halations of the overheated study hall; sometimes it accompanies you to the
dormitory, and even between your sheets, where you can still try to retain its
last atoms before going to sleep. So that now you try, each time you see her,
to fill your nostrils with that fragrance. But the other day, when you thought
Tamara had changed perfume . . . A little tragedy. You didn't dare ask her:
these are intimate things, which it's indecent to talk about. Fortunately, the
following week, you had the pleasure of being greeted, from the moment you
entered her home, by the familiar aroma.

More and more often, rather than listening, you're content to look. The
movement of her lips. That of her eyelids. Of her eyelashes. You're on the
lookout for the moments when her right hand, which she moves while talking to you, will graze one of your wrists. Inadvertently, you believe. But why
shouldn't she be, she too, "absent-mindedly docile for some profound reason,"
as your new favorite poet says of his Young Fate?[26] What does it matter?
You'll have just enough time, then, to feel the warmth of her fingertips on
your naked skin.

You wait for the silences she slips between her sentences: then a slight smile
comes over her face. You don't know how, at those moments, you're able to
conceal your emotion, to act properly, despite the fiery ball that forms deep
in your throat.

In the evening, in the dormitory, your eyes wide open in the half-light, you
mentally inventory what you've succeeded in storing up in the course of these
meetings for which you've prepared yourself as if for a voyage of discovery.
Gestures, looks, attitudes, movements of the body, have been recorded: your
memory takes pleasure in retaining everything, hoarding everything.

Then you thrill in going slowly over her body, noting each of what you
do not hesitate to call, to yourself, her "charms." Like the précieux poets
you feed upon (you've just bought a little anthology of their poems, which
appeared quite recently), you too dream of writing a blason on them. Yes,
soon, when you've learned, through your own experience, what pleasure each
of these "perfections" can give. Ah, secretly, you already feel proud of them.
A pride commensurate with your future triumphs.

When at last you succeed in going to sleep, you don't always sleep well.
You have seen resurfacing, who knows why, some of your childhood nightmares. But other dreams have also appeared. More and more often, you have

to undergo tests whose difficulty daunts you: sometimes you're in cities rather familiar to you, confronted by rows of carefully locked doors you don't know how to get through; sometimes there are gardens surrounded by steep walls at the foot of which you're doomed to wander endlessly; or again you're panting, after a long and exhausting run, at the entry to a grotto blocked by huge stones. Only when you awaken do you realize the extent of the damage.

8

Amaranth

How many times, after nights heavy with desire, nights full of
nightmares or nights of insomnia, Manuel wanted to leave his pretended good behavior behind! To drop the mask he forced himself
to wear when he was around Tamara. To tell his friend how much
their meetings, their laughter, their shared secrets, and especially
the impression of being a couple they gave everyone who saw them
but did not know them, meant to him. To confide to her, for example, how jubilant he was, how he blazed up (inwardly, of course)
as soon as an itinerant photographer, a bohemian, a street vendor,
stopping them on the Boul'Mich, said to them in a loud voice: *This
way, little lovers!*

Each time, he had succeeded in containing his impulses, and had
preferred to postpone. At first, he'd tried to wait for the return of
good weather. He'd feel more at ease then, less out of place. The
higher temperatures, the clarity of the sky, the warmer air would
help untie his tongue: no matter how brief his experience in matters
of love, warmth and the urges of the heart have always gotten on
well together. So he'd been on the lookout, Sunday after Sunday, for
the return of good weather, certain that the decisive hour for him
would arrive with it. But when spring had finally come, Manuel had
still not discovered what he had to do in order to declare his love.

He imagined this declaration—on which he inwardly put the
largest of all capital "D"s—as a stage of the greatest gravity. Nothing
less than a solemn and definitive commitment of both their lives.
From the outset, he'd rejected any idea of a direct declaration. Words
such as "Tamara, I love you more than anything in the world," which
he repeated to himself a hundred times a day, would never have
come out of his mouth; they would have burned his throat. So he
sought other avenues. On the day preceding each of their meetings,

he tried to imagine all the possible turns their conversation might take, in order to find the path that would inevitably lead to confiding and confessing. A labor that occupied his hours of insomnia. At those moments, nothing seemed impossible to him. He knew that his mind was capable of easily solving the enigmas he'd struggled with during the day. Then he saw the questions and answers following one another, in an almost perfect order; he distinguished the main variants; he knew what words to say and what words to avoid. He finally went to sleep, happy to have forged the instrument of his deliverance, of their common deliverance. But the next day, as soon as Tamara opened her mouth, nothing remained of the clever structures he'd built up the previous night. He was obliged, ultimately, to admit his ineptitude in mastering the development of the dialogue, in controlling, even to the slightest degree, its always unforeseeable outpouring.

Furious with himself, he didn't know what to do. He didn't feel capable of imitating his favorite literary heroes, the Frédérics, the Juliens, the Félixes.[27] Those guys! Lovers full of daring, lovers almost always satisfied – everything seemed so simple for them! The most passionate words, and sometimes the most direct, the most explicit gestures came to them easily, without being inhibited by any fear, any kind of reserve! And these words and gestures were received with favor, and even fervor, by those to whom they were addressed, who never thought (or did so rarely, and purely conventionally) of rejecting them, or taking offense at them! He would have liked to belong to that universe! But that grace, obviously, had not been granted him. He told himself that he would certainly have picked up Mme Arnoux's violet-striped shawl, but he would never have dared seize Mme de Rênal's hand; as for going to kiss, while rolling his head on them, the plump white shoulders of Mme de Mortsauf . . .

For a moment, he considered adopting for his own use the procedure that had succeeded so well for Violetta: saying nothing directly, but borrowing from poetry a few carefully selected formulas. For that purpose, he collected a stock of familiar verses, with which he composed this couplet: *Sur votre jeune sein que la blancheur défend / Laisser rouler ma tête à sa proie attachée.*[28] Which he never sent, of course. *"Inappropriate. Absurdly unsuited to the exceptional being that is Tamara!"* Regretfully, he tore the paper to bits.

That did not prevent him from writing a little later on, in a fever – a fever at least equal to that which had gripped him the day after their first meeting – one of those formidable letters in which one allows oneself to be borne along by what one believes are the impulses of the heart and which are often only resurgences of old readings. Everything was there. How he'd fallen in love with her at first sight. How her beauty had overwhelmed, one after the other, all his senses. How for weeks he'd been passing through contradictory states, experiencing in turn desire and fear, hope and shame. He repeated certain phrases, constructed solely with the letters of his beloved's name, which he'd thought up especially to tell her of his love. He even spoke of the secret characters he wanted to invent, which would be the first elements of a language that would belong to them alone. A language in which words, made of shimmering vowels supported by a thin framework of consonants, would flow all by themselves and be only a perpetual invitation to pleasure. But he didn't have the courage to send her this heap of extravagances. He'd recalled one of Larbaud's phrases, and stayed his hand. It seemed to him that he would instantly die of shame if he provoked a reaction analogous to that of the beautiful Fermina, who one day replied to poor Jouanny's frenzied outpouring of feeling, "Monsieur Léniot, why don't you put the gifts God gave you to a better use?"[29]

It was then that the idea of giving her flowers occurred to him. What would be more poetic, after all? With a fond smile, he found in his memory, without really having sought them, bits of the old tune that Ariane used to sing in her high-pitched voice when, still children, they were lingering after their neighborhood school was out, and met someone on the street carrying a bouquet:

Les fleurs sont des mots d'amour
Des mots plus tendres qu'un poème.[30]

But he had no experience in these matters, his much too well regulated love affair with Violetta having never given rise to this kind of offering. Moreover, he knew nothing, or almost nothing, about the world of flowers. Only a few names that pleased him especially by their sonorities (tuberose, begonia, narcissus, bougainvillea) and with whose syllables he liked to play, without worrying about the form, the color, or the fragrance of the plants that might correspond to them. Then, after long hesitation, and after much walking up and down in front of its display window full of dusty green plants, he decided one afternoon to go into a flower shop he'd found in the Rue Le Goff, next to a dressmaker, and which was kept by an old woman who always wore a navy blue apron. He told himself that she would certainly be able to advise him: she must have seen many a lover in difficulty, whom she had surely been able help. She greeted him with a smile, but a smile that he immediately found – without knowing why – more full of irony than of good will. However, he didn't allow himself to be disconcerted, and bravely looking the florist in the eye – and thereby discovering that she suffered from a very slight strabismus – he managed, in a few words, to explain his situation to her. She thought for scarcely an instant, and then suggested, as if what she said were self-evident:

"Well, then . . . You need a nice bouquet of roses. Red roses, of course. And even, I'd say, the red we call . . . amaranth!"

This last word, which she seemed to have intentionally detached, made him tremble. He was immediately seduced by its sonorities. Amaranth: even more than "tuberoses," this word seemed to him to contain, at least in part, the aura of nobility that was appropriate for his future lover.

Sensing that he was rattled, the ancient shopkeeper tried to exploit her advantage. She undertook to explain the symbolic meaning of such a present.

"Ardent love and long-continuing desire," she breathed into his ear.

He immediately began hesitating again. Was this such a good idea, after all? Thinking again with rage about the very sumptuous and very eloquent "poems in flowers" that Félix composed to express his love to Mme de Mortsauf, he feared that the small bouquet (he couldn't afford more than a dozen) he was preparing to have delivered might appear stingy to Tamara. Or, worse yet, because of its meaning, insolent. He backed out of the shop. Pale, sheepish, and especially, once again, empty-handed.

No, decidedly, even the language of flowers, born to express what too blunt words are incapable of saying, was not subtle enough to be appropriate for Tamara. He had to find other means. Invent new ones, if need be. In any case, proceed only with prudence, by discreet, gradual allusions, and only at the opportune moment. He feared above all any sort of improvisation: by revealing himself too soon, he risked rushing the natural course of things, truncating the stages indispensable for maturation.

So he was always looking for a sign, an indication – no matter which – that he could interpret as an encouragement. There was no lack of them. But every time he thought he had one, in a gesture, a smile, a word more full of grace or sweetness, he couldn't help immediately analyzing it. Dissecting it. Sifting it. He called this "my kind of methodological doubt," and he indulged in it with a malign stubbornness, putting all his intellect into it.

No one had taught him the code that would have allowed him to decipher with certainty the behavior of his friend. Hence he mistrusted the formidable propensity he had – or was convinced he had, though Ariane had assured him a hundred times of the contrary – of seizing on the slightest expression of good will and vastly exaggerating its importance. He therefore always ended up finding the flaw. Too fleeting, on coming out of a matinee at the Salle Pleyel, her remark on the refinement of his fingers (ah! *your pianist's fingers*, she'd said, touching them lightly, and it was the first time she'd complimented him, just as Violetta used to do, on a detail of his physique). Too furtive, in the half-light of their special restaurant on the Champs-Elysées, the flutter of her eyelashes in which he might have seen an invitation to be bolder. Too ambiguous, while being tossed around in the metro car, the gesture of her hand lingering on his shoulder, which he'd at first perceived as a modest caress. No question of boasting about such tiny, fragile clues. He needed different kinds of certainties.

And yet, there had been some opportunities he might have seized. Chance, or rather Providence – a beneficent Providence, and not entirely without a sense of humor sometimes – had on several occasions managed to put them in situations suitable for breaking the ice.

The first took place in the Luxembourg Gardens, one afternoon in April. The sky was still dotted with little white clouds, but from time to time an almost warm breath of air accentuated the mildness of the first spring days. Manuel was recounting, with a great many gestures and funny faces, a minor episode in the life of the boarding school: a dispute between first-year students in the course of which one of the monitors – the little shrew-faced man with a mustache to whom he'd taken a dislike on his very first evening there – had managed once again to make himself ridiculous. And Tamara was laughing uninhibitedly. She was laughing with the light laugh he never grew tired of and that he was proud now to be able to elicit whenever he wanted to. Suddenly, in the apparently deserted lane they'd just entered, an unexpected sight forces them to fall silent. A big baby, his lips half-closed, blond and delightfully fat-cheeked, looks at them with curiosity, detaching his mouth from the discreetly bared breast (which is, however, completely visible in its firm and milky roundness, on which the pink of the nipple can even be discerned) of his very young mother. Who has abandoned herself, drowsing in her metal armchair, to the April breeze. She is dressed very lightly for the season. From her wrinkled dress, which reveals the delicacy of each of her limbs, something is sticking out a bit: a fringe of pale lace on the bottom of her slip. What first strikes Manuel, on contemplating this premature nap, is the woman's face. An almost exact copy of Tamara's: the same velvety skin, the same arch of the eyebrows, the same curve of the nose, the same way of keeping her mouth open when she breathes. His imagination is enchanted. He has no difficulty finding points of comparison. The two bodies are soon superimposed. To the point of melting into each other. In a single svelte, fragile silhouette. It is his friend he suddenly sees stretched out at his feet. She's there, Tamara, in this nonchalant attitude so little in accord with her habits, but so full of antique simplicity. She's there, happy in her body and proud of this blooming breast, which she has finally decided to offer to caresses. They're not bold enough, either of them, to comment on this spectacle. Simultaneously, they avert their eyes and leave behind them, indifferent to their passage, under the guard of her little baby, the beautiful sleeper.

Another time, it was in the middle of a little carnival that was being held over by the Place Blanche, on the Boulevard, right near the metro stop. A merry-go-round, a lottery, two shooting galleries, and the inevitable track on which a dozen bumper-cars are noisily crashing into each another, amid sparks and teenagers' laughter. They'd ended up there by chance, having come down from the Place du Tertre. Slowly, they tour the attractions, accompanied by the knowing winks of a few old gypsy women who smile at them with all their gold teeth. They finally stop in front of a strange machine covered from top to bottom with symbols that pretend to be aggressively cabalistic, artlessly mixing pseudo-hieroglyphics, bogus Chinese ideograms, and imaginary Hebrew letters. On the triangular pediment, an inscription in bold capital letters proclaimed something like this:

THE MAGUS ROTOMAGO TELLS YOU YOUR FATE

They immediately saw that for a few francs the machine would deliver, after a slow and rumbling mastication, a little ticket, printed on greenish, poor-quality paper, informing them about the future. Without hesitating, they put a few small coins into the slot. The paper they received bore, in a strange typeface and with many exclamation points, the following words:

> You've been waiting for this moment for such long time!
> Don't wait! Finally say what's in your heart!
> You won't regret it!

They read together, in unison, the message. Disconcerted for a moment, they looked questioningly at each other. Manuel was about to open his mouth when Tamara, folding and then meticulously tearing up the paper, made a handful of confetti of it and threw it away with a little laugh: the minuscule colored fragments flew into the damp air and then fell, scattered, in the gutter. They walked the rest of the way down the boulevard, as far as the bus stop, in silence.

They did not lack even the most traditional, the most classic of the opportunities afforded novice lovers in all the world's legends: the thunderstorm that begins suddenly, with such violence that it obliges the lovebirds to seek refuge in some dark grotto and remain there for a long time, hugging each other, which finally causes their timidity to melt away. For them, this took place during a walk on the island in the Bois de Boulogne, where Tamara had insisted on going despite the threatening storm clouds. They were walking all alone on the path alongside the water. Tamara had just picked up in the grass a minuscule bird's feather when thunder and rain surprised them. Hand in hand, they ran to take shelter at the foot of a great oak tree that rose up ceremoniously on top of a little hill. But the rain came down twice as hard. Manuel took off his coat and put it over Tamara's head, in order to protect her from the big raindrops that splashed her face and wet her hair. She smiled, and, so that the coat could cover both of them, without saying a word she put her head very close to her companion's shoulder. They remained that way for a moment, without even looking at each other, both holding their breath, motionless and huddled together under their improvised canopy. The shower didn't last long.

What caused Manuel's anguish, what paralyzed him all through this period, was his uncertainty regarding Tamara's possible reactions. What if his beloved's feelings were not what he hoped they were? What if she continued to see in him merely a friend, whom she treated with affection, to be sure – and even with the attentive good will that was natural to her – but on whom she did not intend to confer any role other than the one he'd had from the outset: a pleasant and eloquent companion for cultural outings? These fears, hardly formulated, became more specific, expanded, and multiplied. Did he really know her as well as he thought he did? After all, there were whole aspects of her life – her family situation, her friendships, her dreams for the future – that she seldom felt the need to talk to him about. By trying to move beyond this comradeship, which had its own advantages since it allowed him to see her almost as often as he wanted, he was surely going to ruin every-thing: to make himself ridiculous, and especially give his beloved's mother – whom he had glimpsed only once in the half-light of the apartment in the Rue Nicolo, but whose meddling he feared with-out knowing quite why – a pretext for separating him from her, for separating her from him.

Then, out of fear of disappointing his friend, of annoying her, and finally losing her, he preferred to put off expressing his desire, and even to sacrifice, if necessary, a little of his desire. He told him-self, not without bad faith, that perhaps, in his ignorance of these things, he was deceiving himself regarding his own feelings. He cer-tainly diagnosed in himself, and with certitude, an incontestable, deep need to love. But who knows? Perhaps this imperious, tyran-nical need to love had misled him? Perhaps he'd not yet arrived, whatever he thought, at true love? So he continued to keep silent. And so ostentatiously that in the long run his silence, he imagined, would surprise her, or even – why not? – begin to appear to her in its poignant eloquence. Thus he managed to retain the hope that that circumstances would end up changing in his favor, and that his sacrifice was only provisional.

Moreover, all the caresses he didn't dare even to hint at during the daytime, she now came to lavish on him herself under cover of night and sleep. Between dream and reality there remained for him only an infinitesimal distance (that of a single syllable, or even, if one considered the matter still more closely, a simple consonant).[31] Then he had the sensation that he was moving in a world of light-ness and transparency, where he could advance without meeting ob-stacles, without hitches, without effort. There were hours and hours of being face-to-face, tête-à-tête, body to body, mouth to mouth. In perfect harmony, their wedding ceremony took place, impalpable and violent, on a shadowy stage that even the alarm clock's ringing, or the proctor's redoubled blows on the metal edge of the bed, were not able to dissolve. Since his beloved consented to give herself to him in his sleep, he would have liked never to have to open his eyes again.

9

Party

This Sunday, 11 May 1958 (a day always to be remembered).

Finally! This time, I think there is no longer any doubt! Yes! I've got all night, or at least the little that remains of the night, to think about this outing. For I have not, of course, succeeded in going to sleep. I would have liked to write everything down immediately, just as it came to me, last night, on coming home. I still had her scent on me. And that of the vodka. And the taste of the champagne as well. But it was impossible to write in the study hall at such a time. It was after one in the morning, and I would have had the night watchman on my back in five minutes. So I went up to the dormitory. I tried to calm my excitement — well, I believe I can go so far as to call it "elation." How? By reconstituting in detail, in my head, every one of the moments, every one of the details of the evening. And now I'm going to try to repeat them in writing.

It was yesterday, then. For Sophie's eighteenth birthday. Sophie? She's the cousin I'd heard mentioned two or three times. The closest friend of my two dear twins, even though she in no way resembles either of them. Sonia had warned me a long time ago: there would be on this occasion a soirée, half family reunion, half party. "Of course, you're invited. You'll do us the honor of being, once again, our common sigisbée,"[32] she'd said, laughing, for she likes the obsolescence of this word, which she takes pleasure in applying to me every time she gets a chance and which sounds, when she says it, like an exotic aristocratic title. The prospect of being included in a genuine family party, somewhere other than these public places — far too public for my taste — where we usually went, had filled me with joy.

Last Thursday, I called, as agreed, to ask for final instructions. The sweetness of Tamara's voice. She goes directly to the heart of the matter.

"You know, Sonia isn't going to be able to come to the party. She asked me this morning to make her excuses to you. So you'll be escorting only one of us. That doesn't disappoint you too much, I hope?"

She thought she had to console me? I couldn't help seeing in this a little wink. A very good omen. For she, more than anyone, knew that Sonia's absence was not likely to bother me, less than ever on that evening!

"In any case, don't worry. There'll be lots of other people I like. You'll see, we'll have a good time."

I mumbled some reply, and as usual, put a quick end to the conversation. Among the students who were waiting their turn for the telephone, a few, I don't know why, starting making coarse jibes at me as I passed by them. I let them do it. Instead of returning to the study hall, I remained a moment motionless in the corridor, looking down on the courtyard below without seeing it.

I awaited this party with a mixture of hope and fear: a decisive step might be taken, I was sure of it.

Breaking with our habits, we arranged to meet in the apartment where the party was to take place. Somewhere in the sixteenth arrondissement, near the Porte de Saint-Cloud: a quarter that is, along with Passy, I was told the other day, one of the main Russian neighborhoods in Paris, and where I had never yet had occasion to set foot. I went there in a taxi. When I arrived at the address given, I decided, despite my impatience, to walk up and down for a long time in the vicinity of the building. Above all, I didn't want to run the risk of entering, before Tamara, a place where she would be the only one who knew me. It's a fine, brand-new looking building, rather upscale, with a garden full of red roses. Without difficulty, I found, among discreetly illuminated lanes, the right building, the elevator, the floor, and the apartment.

When the time came to ring the bell, I paused for a minute. Several minutes. Something vague, indefinable, held me back. A reawakening of that old fund of timidity that I know only too well. Was I right to accept this invitation? It will be, clearly, a test of my acceptability. Will I be up to it? And what if I make a fool of myself in front of all these people? Knock over a bottle, break a glass, or trip on the carpet, as I did the other night at the dinner at my old philosophy professor's place? These people, who've moved easily in this world that has always been their own, won't they notice, at first glance, my awkwardness as an intruder? And, worst of all, won't they, with Tamara looking on, laugh behind my back at the embarrassment evident in every one of my gestures? But, I immediately told myself, that wasn't the only reason I was procrastinating before the door. I was on the point of committing a serious act that was going to give, in the presence of all her relatives and friends, a public, official character to my relationship with Tamara. Something like an engagement, in short. That was well worth a moment of reflection.

I ended up surmounting my fear. I didn't want to be found, either, by new arrivals, in the absurd position — my hand raised, the index finger glued to the button — in which my reverie had kept me. Moreover, I'd begun to perceive, through the door, laughter, Russian music, loud voices: apparently, the guests were there, the party was well underway. I made up my mind to ring. It was Tamara who opened the door. Tamara, radiant in a very simple, light green silk dress that revealed most of her shoulders and the beginning of her breasts.

"Ah, there you are! Do you know you're very late?"

Raising her voice somewhat, and pointing her index finger at me, she pretended to scold me. But the twinkle in her eyes and the generous laugh that followed these words helped me relax.

"Now, I got here a good half an hour before everyone else. Because of you, of course. You're always so punctual!"

She immediately slips her hand into mine and leads me toward Sophie, who greets me without formality.

"Welcome, welcome! So you're Manuel, Sonia's famous friend?"

"He's my friend, too, a little bit," Tamara immediately corrects her. "And even, for this evening, mine alone, aren't you?"

"Well, you've certainly made people want to meet you! You didn't have too much trouble getting here, at least? Obviously, from your Latin Quarter, it's quite a hike . . ." (I omit the rest of this conversation, which is without interest in relation to everything that will follow).

We went together into the large living room, very smartly furnished and brightly lit. About thirty guests, all of whom seem to be about my age. I notice with a pang of envy a few navy blue blazers with gilt buttons, so much more appropriate than my ancient double-breasted jacket. But I also see, with pleasure, one or two nearly naked backs and a couple of charming décolletés (less charming, however, than Tamara's). Little groups of three or four have formed, talking, laughing, drinking off in one gulp little glasses of an unfamiliar vodka, whose scent of wild herbs goes up my nostrils and stays with me for a long time.

Tamara knows everyone, of course. She takes me from one person to another. The round of first names, pronounced sometimes in the Russian fashion, sometimes in the French, quickly makes me dizzy.

"Vladimir, Nicolas, they're studying medicine, they met at the Fac."

"Olga and Oleg. One might say they were made for each other. Anyway, they're planning to get married."

"Ah, here's Tatiana, Vladimir's sister. She's preparing to study literature at the Sorbonne. She's a little lost. She may need to call on you for help, if you're willing, before the exams."

I mumble "of course, I'd be glad to help," and smile broadly at Tatiana, whose very pretty green eyes are already looking elsewhere.

"Natasha, Dimitri, they're at Sciences Po,[33] and Sasha, who's just behind there, is too."

"Irina, a cousin. She's fearless, she wants to be an actress."

I smile. I shake hands. I try to retain the first names, to stamp the faces on my memory. I say to myself: "So these are people I'm going to end up seeing from now on, with her. I have to inform myself a little better about this milieu, I have to adapt to it. It'll be easy, if she helps me." Apparently Tamara has already talked about me to some people. And those, it seems to me, greet me with more warmth. With curiosity, too. They ask me questions. About Louis-le-Grand, about Morocco, about my options for the future. I talk about the Rue d'Ulm,[34] teaching, writing. I prudently add that all that is still very uncertain.

"Less uncertain than he thinks!" quickly adds Tamara, who is directing the conversation with an ease and an authority I've not seen in her before, since I've never seen her in a group.

Part of the evening was thus spent making the rounds of the various little groups, to satisfy their curiosity, to participate in their laughter. I don't know how long that might have lasted. The joy of feeling Tamara constantly very close to me, her eyes bigger and more brilliant than ever, her left hand lingering at times on my forearm, made me lose all idea of time. I see only one thing: amid all these people who have been her friends far longer than I have—some of them since she was a child—and who seem to have for her a very special devotion, she makes every effort not to leave me for a single instant. In what she says, I'm well aware, even when she's not addressing me directly, that it's for me that she's talking. Every time she can, she repeats

76

some of my words, some of my expressions, and thus gives me the pleasure of finding in her speech a sort of echo of my own.

At a certain moment, the Russian music gave way to American. A few couples got up to dance. And we followed their example. Without hesitating, without reticence. The most natural thing in the world. But it was the first time. Yes, until yesterday, our common activities had been exclusively "intellectual," not to say "cerebral." Well, then, dancing together, there, in the middle of all those people! That meant we were finally remembering our bodies; we no longer ignored them, we were even capable of making of them, for a few instants, a means of pleasure. A completely new pleasure. As legitimate, as avowable, as all the others. A real revolution!

Every time the rhythm of the music seemed to us right (we left to a few fanatics the wild agitation and wriggling of bebop and rock and roll, and patiently waited for the slow dances), we got up together to join the other couples. People moved out of our way. They smiled at us. Only the previously mentioned Vladimir, who did not dance even once in the course of the evening (except with his very charming sister) was looking at us, it seemed to me, without good will. Tamara's two arms were wound very naturally around my body, her forehead sometimes resting on my shoulder. I had right against me the body that, a few hours earlier, had seemed to me the most inaccessible in the world. Our steps were not exactly the same as those of the other dancers. She hardly cared, and I cared still less. Very quickly, we succeeded in giving our movements a rhythm, always the same, repeated over and over, that had nothing to do with the piece being played. I didn't even need to lead her. One and the same impulse drove us, dictated our movements. The slowing or accelerating of the music around us had disappeared into the distance. There remained only a sort of ecstasy, which had slowly overtaken us both.

At the stroke of midnight the birthday cake was brought in. Enormous, and completely covered with a layer of crème blanche sprinkled with tiny bits of candied fruit. The lights were turned off. Surprised, I had instinctively squeezed Tamara's hand, which had not left mine since the last dance. Sophie comically puffed out her cheeks and managed to blow out in a single breath the eighteen little white candles. A barrage of Russian words — some of them repeated in unison by all the guests — rang out amid laughter and applause. After which, with the hubbub still going on, a few bottles of champagne were opened. On the tray Vladimir presented to us with a mock bow, Tamara, after a very brief instant of reflection, took only one glass, the fullest. She immediately gave it to me. Then, in the voice that lent a magical resonance to her slightest words, she murmured (and I thought I saw, at that moment, her lower lip quiver):

"Shall we share?"

"If you wish, yes."

"You drink first."

"All right."

"Well, go ahead! What are you waiting for?"

"Yes, yes. But if I do, you're going to know everything I think!"

"Oh, well, I believe [a rather long pause], I believe . . . I already know a little, don't I?"

As she said that, she put, in a rapid movement, a finger on her lips, which the vodka had very lightly moistened. As if to tell me that there was nothing else to say. And I thought I saw in her eyes, at that instant, something that seemed to me an offering. But as soon as she had understood that I'd seen this look, she got hold of herself. Her smile became more timid: it now seemed addressed only to herself.

When the champagne had been drunk, and after a bit of racket and general excitement, the atmosphere of the party began to calm. Most of the guests started getting ready to leave. Caught up in the round of good-byes, on several occasions Tamara had to leave me alone with her cousin. Then she told me it was time for her, too, to go home. Vladimir and his sister would give her a ride in their car.

Thus this evening ended: long and full like an adventure, and ultimately hardly less brief than a dream. I took from Sophie's place an ineffable impression. Simultaneously carried away, swept up, invaded by a current that submerged me. Walking off alone in search of a taxi, I was floating in a soft haze. As if drunkenness had interposed between external objects and my eyes a stream of downy clouds.

Without quite knowing how, I found myself going down the Lycée's corridors, entering the study hall, dark and empty. During the evening I'd not thought, even for an instant, of this gray place that has been the framework of my existence for months. Now I looked on it with complete scorn. No, nothing would ever take away from me the moments that I'd just lived through: not the dirty walls, nor the floor covered with stains, nor the tables still sticky with the residues of food left by the residents' snack, nor the blackboard bearing its daily load of graffiti of an erudite obscenity (today: "les cénobites tranquilles").[35] Nothing will ever take away from me the moments I've just relived.

One regret: there's no one here to whom I can tell all this. Fabrice, good old Fabrice, where are you? It's true, I've forgotten you a little during this blissful spring. But now, I would so much like to talk to you about her. Or simply to hear myself talk about her . . . Too bad, I'll console myself when I send my weekly letter to my sister. But I know that this time, once again, I won't tell her everything. She probably wouldn't understand.

10

Mornings After

Don't smile too much, please, mocking reader, at the sweet turmoil of this young man of long ago. I willingly grant that it's not exactly how things would happen and be said these days. But what do you expect? I've not dared add anything, or cut anything, from these pages, which were only too obviously composed nonstop, under the influence of euphoria. If you're someone who likes unedited documents, slices of life, authenticity, there you have it! As for feelings . . . You should just know that if you haven't yourself been through such things at least once (they're difficult to believe only for those who've never experienced them), you have all my sympathy.

With that party, a threshold, which I hoped was decisive, had been crossed toward a relationship more in accord with my wishes and – I was then completely sure – with Tamara's as well. By her attitude, from the first minute to the last, she'd anticipated all my desires, fulfilled all my expectations. With one small exception, however. A minuscule incident, which I had (by an innocent ruse of the unconscious?) left out of my written account.

It happened as we were leaving, just before I separated from Tamara. Spurred by the most natural, the most spontaneous of impulses, I had without thinking put my hands on her bare shoulders and, with my eyes closed, drawing her gently toward me, in a movement that nothing could have halted, I had begun to bring her mouth to mine. She showed no surprise, did not pull away, made not even the slightest resistance. I was expecting a kiss, then, one of those long, subtly meandering kisses with elaborate sinuosities, a kiss sweeter and more intense than anything I'd been able to experience up to that point with casual partners, a kiss that would be the crowning moment, the reward (in my view, wholly deserved!) for the weeks of waiting and hoping that had prepared it. But I got only a rapid, ethereal, almost fraternal peck, which even managed, by some incomprehensible last-minute deviation, to avoid my opened lips, and lightly planted itself somewhere low on my left cheek, which was still burning. It certainly did not resemble the robust hugs and kisses in the Russian fashion that other people, at the same moment, at the other end of the living room . . .

I had no choice but to leave immediately afterward, without saying a word, without even a last exchange of looks with Tamara, taking with me only this too flimsy trophy. At first, the incident annoyed me, but on reflection, it ended up moving me. I refused to see in our strange kiss – improvised, clumsy, and incomplete, to be sure, but exchanged without embarrassment and in front of everyone – anything other than a discreet anticipation, a modest initial version, of all those that would soon follow it and of which it was, in short, only the precursor, the herald. It was normal, after all, that with Tamara things had happened this way: it was only too obviously her first experience. But there was no question of leaving it at that. So in the middle of my classes on history or philosophy, or in the evening, in the dormitory, after the lights were put out, I began to dream about our next rendezvous. The day would soon come when Tamara's lips would no longer go astray, when her mouth would know how to find mine, her breath join with mine. When she herself would be, in my arms, only a blaze of kisses, and kisses that would be, from then on, the emanation of her whole body. In such moments, the memory of Violetta, whom I had succeeded in almost completely forgetting since I'd fallen in love with Tamara – simply mentioning their names in the same breath seemed to me blasphemous – resurfaced. Violently. And this memory no longer shocked me.

Therefore I waited with confidence. With curiosity, too. I was trying to guess what means my very modest beloved was going to use to send me the message that now had to be sent: that we had entered a new phase in our relationship, that the step we had taken was irrevocable, that we were finally going to be able to talk about our love, to show it, and, especially, to live it. I imagined her embarrassed by an exercise so new to her: she hesitated, sought the most appropriate

81

words, circumlocutions, experimented with understatement and metaphor, or else, to get around the difficulty, perhaps even thought of slipping in – as she sometimes did in her asides to Sonia – some formula that sounded foreign (Russian, but also English, being for both of them the privileged instruments of confession, effusion) in which her avowal would be discreetly couched. I also wondered how much time she would need to make up her mind. Just as I had, she must have, already on Sunday morning, begun to assess the situation. Why would she have been less impatient than I was? It was she, who by her unambiguous attitude, had launched the new course of things. I couldn't imagine that she hadn't done it intentionally.

I was almost sure that she would decide to send me, as early as the beginning of the following week, a *pneumatique*. I had already told her how much I liked this kind of message, and the scenes for which it was the pretext in the boarding school. So I took the precaution, even before my history class on Monday morning (the one in the middle of which I had more than once, on certain winter days, fallen asleep), of going to see dear old Eugène (called Hugène, called Gégène, called The Gross), to inform him that he was to transmit to me without delay the very urgent message that my sister, who was visiting Paris (I was not going to let this old drunk in on the – sacred – secret of my love affair, after all!) was going to send me. And immediately afterward, just to be sure, I began to keep an eye, through the windows of the classroom, on the comings and goings, several times a day, of the porters in white shirts who were entrusted with distributing the regular mail. Every time I glimpsed the silhouette of one of them at the end of a corridor, I immediately thought I saw rising up at the same time thousands of them, bearing thrilling messages signed "your beloved," and I had forcibly to restrain my desire to run up to them. Then I threw myself into examining (it would be very excessive to call it reading) three heavy volumes on the history of Russia I'd just borrowed from the library.

The days of the week thus wore on, one by one. No message came. Fear began to show its face. As usual, I found no other way of calming my malaise than to describe it.

Friday morning, 16 May 58: a note written during D.'s class on "the experience of time" (I didn't make that up, alas!).

Decidedly, it was written that you would have to do your whole apprenticeship in a single season. The evil genius (him again!) who conceived the plan of your accelerated sentimental education has not been idle. Any more than he lets you be idle. On your program, from now on, he has put the agony of waiting. It's true that a few foretastes had already been vouchsafed you: for example, when, on a certain Saturday evening, in front of the Trocadero theater, you had to wait anxiously, a good half an hour, for Tamara, not knowing from which exit she was going to emerge; or another time—contrary to the usual rule, it was a Thursday, late in the afternoon—at the Saint-Lazare train station, in the waiting room, when, motionless among the double stream of hurried travelers, some running from the metro to the train, others from the train to the metro, amid noise and indifference, you spent an interminable hour envisaging the most terrible hypotheses explaining your friend's lateness, before realizing, on seeing her suddenly emerge smiling from the crowd, that it was you who had been mistaken about the time. But those were only trifles, simple preparatory exercises before the test. This time, on the contrary, you're really getting into the subject.

None of the books you've read, none of the classes you've taken had yet allowed you to understand anything about time, about lived time. Especially not the class whose main point you're right now in the process of missing, and which opened, inevitably, with Saint Augustine's sempiternal Quid enim est tempus? But now you're capable of giving a very personal response to that excessively famous question. For, thanks to the experience that the past week has been for you, you know. You know the immensity of what can be enclosed within even the briefest moment. You know about those instants that subdivide themselves infinitely, into minuscule particles, more and more minuscule, but always just as clearly distinct from each other. You know to what each of them owes its autonomy, its integrity, to the fact that it is marked by the feeling of absence. And by the hope, renewed from moment to moment, that this absence will cease.

On Sunday morning, my internal agitation reached its climax. I didn't know what to do. Telephone? I didn't dare. In fact, up to that point, I'd never called Tamara, just as earlier I'd never called Sonia, except on the days and at the times that they themselves had told

83

me, with great precision, to call. The fear of embarrassing her by calling at the wrong time held me back. So I wrote a very short note, which expressed, as simply as possible, my surprise, my increasingly intense concern, my need to be reassured as soon as possible, and my immense affection.

The wait began again.

Another week.

Nothing.

With a heavy heart, I sent a second letter. A real call for help, this time. I begged Tamara to tell me the truth, the whole truth, whatever it might be. I wouldn't blame her for any pain her admissions might cause me. But I had to have, right away, some word from her . . .

This letter remained just as unanswered as the preceding one.

I was hurt, alternately panic-stricken and distraught. My divagations at the time are strongly marked by this.

End of May, 58 (notes written during the class on La Nouvelle Héloïse).[36]

Look out! Danger! The whole of your relationship to things is now upset by this affair. Professors, classmates, courses, assignments, lectures, everything that has constituted, since your arrival here, whether you like it or not, the reality around you, is being shifted into the background or simply disappearing altogether. The most tangible objects, even your books, are losing their solidity, the most mechanical actions are revealing themselves as empty of meaning. One thing, only one, concerns you: understanding what has caused to fall upon you, in such an unexpected way, a disgrace like this. The Tarpeian rock is never far away[37] *. . . But all the same!*

You're constantly considering various hypotheses. Absurd, all of them. You reject them, one after another, and then reconsider them, reject them again, and so on. But what can she reproach you for? You don't feel guilty of anything, you aren't *guilty of anything. Except perhaps of that unforeseen urge that, at the party, had drawn you toward her lips. But wasn't that normal, natural, at the end of such an evening? Hadn't she done everything to make you feel secure, closer to her, more intimately united with her, than ever? Let's grant, however, that it is this innocent attempt at a kiss that shocked her. Should she punish you by this silence, of whose cruelty she cannot be unaware, after your two letters? An excessive, disproportionate reaction . . . No!*

No, really! The woman you know, the one whom you immediately trusted, the one who's been haunting you for weeks, is not capable of acting in this way. She's well aware that a single word, or even, simply the slightest sign of her disapproval would have sufficed to return you, if that was what she wanted, to the innocence of your first outings together.

So it must be something else. An incident unrelated to her intentions. Her letter went astray. A distracted messenger forgot it at the bottom of his mailbag: there's such a mass of mail arriving every morning in this damned school! Some idiotic trick played by one of your classmates, who made off with it, not imagining its importance: there are precedents for that, alas! Or else your own letter was lost. Both your letters. Not very likely, all the same. Unless. Unless someone around her diverted both of them, one after the other, in order to create an irreparable misunderstanding between you. Yes, but who? Sonia? Well, why not? What do you know, after all, about the true feelings of these charming girls regarding you? Why would Sonia let her friend Manuel be taken away from her without reacting? Maybe she thinks she has rights to you? Such little jealousies, such sinuous machinations, such secret reprisals are not rare, it's said, among girls, even in the best society. Remember that dark story of Balzac's in which such a diversion of mail succeeded in breaking up, in a short time, a marvelous love affair. But no, all that, once again, is absurd. It's all unthinkable. Radically. You're not in a novel, you're in life, yes, get that into your head, my dear Manuel, in your life, still unstained by any villainy.

So, what then? Well, the truth is that she's been forbidden to write to you. Yes, that's it. Her mother has surely been informed, by some charitable soul, of what happened at the party. That big lout Vladimir, for example. Yes, the medical student. Just between us, what a mug that guy has! He really looks like the villain in a melodrama. It wouldn't be surprising if he'd tattled! He looked pretty furious when he saw you with Tamara. The way he looked at you when you were dancing! Maybe he loves her, too. He must love her. How could he not love her? And for much longer than you have, since, as you could see, all these good people seem to have known each other since they were babies. So, a classic case of jealousy with regard to a successful rival. There's nothing more malicious. The mother, alerted by this cretin, is worried about the way things are going. Ah, I can hear her from here, the good, saintly Russian mother, who zealously watches over the interests of her beloved daughter. "We're not going to let our Tamara act like that in public with this boy, after all. We hardly know him. Where does he come from? What sort of future does he have? No one knows anything about him. And as generous as she is, she could end up getting really attached to him. Then we'd be in a pretty fix! It's high time to put a stop to this, high time." All that seems make sense, alas. It's well known, at least since Shakespeare: there's nothing like the harsh law of the family to destroy a love affair.

But if that's the truth, what a disaster! My poor friend, what sort of wasp's nest have you gotten into? A little world in which people observe each other, are jealous of each other, denounce each other, eliminate each other. With compliments, smiles, filled cakes, and glasses of champagne. I'm ashamed for them. And still more for her, if she accepts all that.

But no, think a minute! You can't, you won't believe that, either. That can't be the solution. Well, then? The only solution that remains is this one, the most banal, the most prosaic: she's forgotten you. Let's say, in order to preserve the favorable image of her that you want to keep, at all costs, momentarily forgotten. Relegated to a far corner of her memory, a corner she no longer has any desire to visit for the time being. Yes, it's as simple as that. Inconstancy? Capriciousness? Affective instability? Not at all. Why do you want to use such big words? A little attack of amnesia, that's all. That happens often enough, it seems, in young women from good families. Nothing like it for getting rid of an admirer who has become too importunate. It doesn't even require any special effort. They go to sleep one night in their soft little beds, and, without knowing how, the next morning they've cleaned out their tender little hearts. Finished, Manuel! Struck off the program for this year! Because of his archaism, he's obviously unsuited to the needs. Clear the decks! Bring in the next one. Anyway, just between us, you're not far from thinking she's right. Who are you then, my dear Manuel, that she should remember you? What exploits have you achieved up to this point that you should claim to occupy the memory of such a distinguished creature? So acknowledge, honestly, your fiasco. What conclusions should be drawn from it? One and one only: react like a man. Get a grip on yourself. You can't accept remaining one more day in this state.

These virtuous final injunctions remained, of course, dead letters. In reality, it was with the greatest difficulty that I succeeded, eventually, in diminishing my rage and moderating my sorrow, the one constantly reawakening the other. Sometimes, both of them made me fall into a somber irony. When everything goes wrong, I read somewhere, there always remains one solution: laugh about it. So, for a day or two, raillery, derision, sarcasm came to sweep everything away: my simple-minded illusions, my naïveté appeared to me in the most clownish light. If Ariane were to see me!

Fortunately, the political turmoil of the second week in May – discreetly referred to as "the events in Algiers" – came just in time to serve me as a distraction, at least for a few days. I'd paid little attention at first. Not even when, one Thursday evening, crossing the Place de la Concorde on the way back from an exhibit on the Avenue Matignon, I found myself, to my great surprise, nose to nose with several rows of uniforms (whether they were policemen or CRS,[38] I don't know) surrounding the Palais-Bourbon. The incident hardly bothered me at all: my concerns were elsewhere. However, the repercussions of the events soon reached the Lycée. With an undeniable intensity. For it seemed to us that what had suddenly perturbed the routine of our little universe was not simply politics and its games, but in fact the current of history.

There was a lot of excitement, really a lot, among the residents. The whole khâgne wanted to consider itself on alert. Everyone considered it his duty to pick up here and there – on the radio, from well-placed relatives – the slightest bits of information. These were then communicated feverishly, during the recreation periods, which were unduly prolonged, and, a sign of the gravity of the situation, prolonged with impunity. From one night to the next, the news got more and more disturbing. Thousands of paratroopers were preparing to descend on Paris. A powerful dictatorship was going to be established by the generals in Algiers. All this was being secretly directed by de Gaulle, in person and with a little clique of conspirators who'd not found any other way of returning to power. In short, the republic, once again, was in danger. At one point, it even seemed that the courses might be canceled and the Lycée closed. The next day, abandoning the classrooms in an atmosphere of mobilization, we fraternized noisily in the hallways with a large number of professors and monitors. Some of them, to whom I had up to then thought political matters were completely alien, surprised me by the vigor and sincerity of their commitment. At least one of them mentioned, with a gravity that impressed me, his past as a resistance fighter, and said he was ready to fight again to defend freedom. The others approved.

Could I, in the midst of this effervescence, simply remain there, inactive, apathetic, paralyzed by my wretched heartaches? No, of course not. So I got involved along with the others. Without measure or reservation, which brought me a little closer still to my classmates, who were glad to see me on their side in these troubled times.

At each new demonstration, we left the Lycée in a group to march from the Bastille to the Place de la République. We sang, together with thousands of others, the "Marseillaise," and I had at those moments the feeling that I was melting, a lump in my throat, into the great, vibrating body that was occupying the street. We all shouted against the dissidents in Algiers, repeating over and over that fascism would not pass. We ran together when the crowd was dispersed, Michel and Gustave seeing to it that I was not left behind, to avoid the policemen's batons. Finally, we went home together, dirty, exhausted, and happy to have so powerfully contributed to the salvation of the republic. A sort of comradeship in arms developed that was not to be without consequences, and that still today gives a certain "veterans" aspect to some of our after-dinner conversations. But soon all this agitation calmed down. To my great stupefaction, de Gaulle took over power very peacefully: new institutions were going to give birth to a new republic . . .

For me, the time of demonstrations had hardly ended when less exciting concerns appeared. The date of the practice exam, to prepare for the one on which admission to khâgne would depend, was now quite near. I had to get ready for it. By continuing to ruminate on my sorrows, I was running the risk of wasting my whole year. What a humiliation that would be! Good reasons for ridding myself of the memory of the unfaithful, inconstant Tamara. Pay her back in her own coin. A memory lapse for a memory lapse. Yes, forget her. But forget her by devoting myself to my work, of course. Resume the stern, indispensable routine of academic exercises.

So I threw myself, along with Michel and Gustave, to whom I had obviously said nothing about my recent disappointments, into orgies of Greek and Latin. Pages and pages of the orators, poets, and philosophers, gone through day after day with great strides. And this lasted, without a break, until the middle of June.

11

Vacation

A particularly warm early afternoon, in mid-June, 1958

The study hall, abandoned by at least half of its usual occupants, had remained strangely silent when good old Eugène (called Hugène, called Gégène, called The Gross) stumbled in. Not the slightest beginning of a racket, not a single obscene song, not even a hoot to welcome him, this man who so placidly and unhurriedly brought the most urgent messages. Like the others, Manuel was dozing. He hadn't gotten beyond the twentieth *dizain* of *Délie*,[39] which was on his reading list for that day.

He no longer expected anything from Tamara. Really nothing. Weeks had gone by. Four, to be precise. Despite his determination to forget everything, he'd not been able to help counting them, halfday after half-day, according to the rhythm of the distribution of the mail. An eternity.

The two letters he'd sent had remained without a reply. He'd drawn the conclusions that seemed to him inevitable. Conclusions that varied from one moment to another. This whole thing, from the beginning, was a dream. A dream that was too beautiful. In which he'd made the great mistake of believing too long. No surprise that the dream had evaporated. The whole thing, from the beginning, was a godsend. A marvelous godsend. Of which he'd made the great mistake of not taking advantage in time. No surprise that another man had grabbed it. Of course, he was angry with Tamara for having toyed with him, but he reproached himself far more for his own naïveté, for his own ineptness.

And then, suddenly, the unexpected happened. Yes, in the torpor of that afternoon, a letter. Or rather, in the slim, pale blue envelope wrinkled by the hazards of transmission, with its profusion of stamps and postmarks, a *pneumatique!* Manuel immediately recognized the writing and couldn't repress a cry of joy, which made a few sleepy heads pop up, at the end of the hall.

The message was brief, but it gave all the explanations he could have wished for. For a month, Tamara had been in the hospital. It had begun the day after the party. During this whole time, she'd seen no one, communicated with no one, not even Sonia. Fortunately, she now felt much better. The two letters he'd sent in May had just been given to her. She was very sincerely moved. She thanked him for thinking of her and urged him not to worry so much from now on. She promised to see him again, of course, as soon as possible. And finally, she assured him of her faithful and deep affection.

Manuel was bubbling with joy. So that was it! Only that! Obviously, the right hypothesis was the simplest one, which, in his dreadful distress, he'd forgotten to consider: illness. A sudden, unexpected illness that had forced his unfortunate friend to remain isolated and silent for several weeks. How could he not have thought of that? But also, how could he have imagined Tamara ill? Radiant and pure, she seemed to him invulnerable, the very incarnation of health! He was now so happy to know, to understand what had happened during those dismal weeks that he didn't for an instant think of asking what this sudden illness was.

What did it matter, since it was all over? He was angry at himself, at this point, for having been capable of doubting his beloved: he couldn't forgive himself for having gone so far as to imagine that she had weaknesses so absurdly incompatible with what he knew of her. The only excuse he could come up with was that he had been led astray by his excessive grief. In reality, all during those dark days, he'd doubted, even more than Tamara, himself.

Naturally, he replied at once: he told his friend how relieved he felt on receiving her letter, this letter he no longer dared expect, and how much he wanted to see her as soon he could. A few days later, she left the clinic, and immediately let him know. But it was impossible for them to meet. She had to leave Paris right away with her mother.

Very quickly, the time of his exams arrived. Relieved, his mind now at peace, he went into them with redoubled vigor. As a result, everything went well. He was admitted to khâgne and even won a few prizes. Then it was time for vacation. He had planned nothing, organized nothing. So, without enthusiasm, he decided to return to Morocco, as his family wanted him to do.

He repeated in reverse, stage by stage, the trip he'd made the preceding fall. The train to Marseilles (with a reserved seat!). A whole, hot day, which gave him the pleasure of contemplating, for the first time, a France everywhere luminous, and as if inexhaustibly flooded with sunlight: he was almost constantly in ecstasy over the sight of it. The next day, at the port, he boarded, not the Djenné, but rather the Koutoubia, for a peaceful voyage to Casablanca. He enjoyed, as a habitué, the crowded bars and decks, which he was even able to liven up with a few late-night tête-à-têtes with two very young and very willing English coeds who were titillated by the sea breeze, the stars, and the full moon that had all obligingly joined them. Finally, the debarkation, at high noon, in the humidity of Casablanca, and the long hug with Ariane, who had been waiting for him on the dock since morning.

After a year like the one he'd just lived through, filled with so many events, so many emotions (he promised himself he would soon write it all down, using the notes he'd taken), how was he going to deal with this return home?

To tell the truth, he had scarcely any illusions regarding the satisfactions – entirely relative – that he was going to derive from it. He was well aware that he was no longer quite the same. Certainly, someone who closely resembled him and who spoke in his name would continue to play his role in family gatherings, or during outings with old friends. They would do their best to fête him, "the university student," "the Parisian." They would help him amuse himself, he'd surely earned that. The resources of the little seaside resort, near Rabat, where his vacation would be spent (it was called Témara!) would be very methodically exploited. They would spend whole days swimming in the Ocean. They would meet almost every evening for dinners of brochettes or grilled fish. Then they would go dancing in one or another of the two local dives, pompously called ballrooms. And in the wee hours of the morning they would devour the big, piping hot fritters, with the light, crispy crust, which they all knew were his favorite treat. But he would now take only a limited pleasure in all these diversions. Even the fantastic mountain landscapes his friends would arrange to set before his eyes, in the course of long car trips in the Atlas range, would leave him almost unmoved. His thoughts would be elsewhere. His deep self, his true self (as he liked to say now) would have remained back there, and he would experience this summer as a long intermezzo, marked principally by waiting. But he would console himself by thinking that at least this wait was very different from all the others he'd known up to that point, less burdened with anguish and uncertainty.

Tamara had told him that she would spend most of the summer with her mother on the Breton coast, just outside Vannes. He'd hardly arrived in Morocco before he wrote to her. He was impatient to erase the memory of the troubled period they had both traversed. What he wanted, now that he knew she was well again, was for things between them to start up again at the precise point where they'd remained blocked: at the kiss that had closed the party at Sophie's place, and which should have opened a new phase in their relationship. Of course, he did not dare to speak of it directly. "It's up to her to repair the rift," he said to himself in private. Naturally, she didn't do that at all. In her letters, Tamara made not the slightest allusion to the party, and still less to the kiss. So it was written that that evening, on which he had based so many hopes, was to remain without consequences. As if the time during which she was sick had served only to abolish the memory of those moments. To the point that he asked himself, sometimes, whether the party had really taken place, if he hadn't simply dreamed it, as he had many other things in his life. At such moments, he congratulated himself on the happy inspiration that had led him to write down without delay, the following morning, a detailed account. When he left the Lycée, he'd put these precious pages in his suitcase, along with all Tamara's letters and *pneumatiques*. He now carried them with him everywhere, and reread them out loud to himself in moments of despondency.

So there now began between them a regular correspondence, but one that took neither the form nor the tone he initially wanted to give it. Out of discretion, no doubt (a discretion he allowed himself, at least once, to tell her he found excessive), Tamara told him rather little about herself or her activities. When she happened to do so (accounts of going by herself to Belle-Île, of a very lively picnic at Houat with Sonia and two cousins who were visiting), she took pleasure above all in noting the perpetually changing form of the clouds over the beach, the strong scent of the rocks after a rain, a leaning pine to which wisteria clung, a pond overtaken by aquatic plants. But her interest seemed to focus, more and more, on Morocco and on Africa. "How lucky you are to have been born down there, to have lived down there!" she repeatedly told him. Or again: "I'm sure your native country resembles you. All contrasts. Proud and gentle at the same time." She had no idea how much this kind of remark pained him, upset him. "Is it possible that she misunderstands me to that degree?"

He had an instinctive distrust of talk that established too close – too mechanical, he said – a relationship between a person and his origins. With a very juvenile assurance, he claimed that he owed only to himself each of his character traits, each of the choices that were soon going to give form to his life. All that, of which he had hardly spoken to her earlier, except by brief, enigmatic allusions, Tamara took some time to understand. She sensed that his relationship to what she had one day called his exotic component ("but don't worry, I sometimes feel very exotic myself," she had immediately added) was difficult, even painful at times. The way he'd replied to the first questions she asked him about Morocco left little doubt on this point.

He could have given a loving description of his native city, which would have suddenly risen up before her, shimmering against a background of an incessantly blue sky, in the interlacing of its gardens, its ochre ramparts, its overcrowded squares, its mosaic-decorated fountains, its souks, its cupolas and its minarets. But immediately turning his back on this parade of conventional images, he'd attacked with repressed – but still very perceptible – rage both the noble picturesque of painters like Delacroix and Matisse and that –

far more suspect – of writers like Loti and the Tharaud brothers (he hadn't dared leave in his letter the derisive formula he'd initially written: the Delatisses and the Macroix, the Lotauds and the Thari). He told her only about the Berber camps, herds of goats or sheep wandering amid scraggly bushes, steep paths hanging amid rocks, or the dry cold of the winter in houses without heating, the feeling of loneliness and distance from the real world, and especially the secret anxiety that pursued him even in his dreams.

At first, she seemed to accept his arguments. Later on, she tried again, and wanting to encourage him, despite everything, she sought to remind him of all the people – painters and writers, but also monks and mystics – who had found themselves by going to Africa. He willingly agreed, but found it rather hard to explain to her why what might have been for others, quite legitimately, a liberating factor, had been for him only a hindrance, for he could find in it neither the sweetness people ordinarily attribute to their native country nor the vengeful stimulation they derive from being uprooted.

To this exchange, Manuel devoted a large part of his time and thought. But the more the letters became, on both sides, serious and based on arguments, sometimes taking the form (which had become natural to both of them) of genuine little essays, the less he felt courageous enough to slip into them, even in the form of an innocent quip, the slightest allusion to what mattered most to him, his overflowing love.

With his old friends, things also went in a way that hardly satisfied him. To be sure, all the promised amusements were there. In great abundance. From swimming to fritters. And a friend Ariane had just made, whom they met as if by accident on their first Sunday at the beach, had even invited him, on several August afternoons, to keep her company for long periods in her parents' cool house. But what he hadn't foreseen, and what caused him the most pain, were the constant questions he was asked about his love life. For his friends, it was more than curiosity, it was an obsession: they imagined him exhausted by the easy but sumptuous opportunities Paris offered, and repeatedly asked him to tell them about his conquests.

He couldn't help, one evening, talking frankly about the affair – the only real one, as he saw it – in which he was currently involved. His listeners were dumbfounded. Really, such a lot of fuss! Such play-acting! An odd bird he'd found! But in a city like Paris, there must certainly be, thank God, lots of less complicated girls. Who were only after that, moreover. Oh, yes, Swedish girls . . . Or Germans . . . Oh, German girls! In the dorm rooms at the Cité Universitaire . . . It seems they go at it hot and heavy . . . Real little bombshells . . . Now if only he would take things in hand, instead of letting himself be manipulated! He found it hard to accept the advice and the re-proaches of those who ("man to man, old pal, man to man, really!"), wanted to warn him. Their inept suggestive remarks, as well, stuck in everywhere. But he wouldn't have tolerated from them the slight-est allusion to Tamara's body. To all this verbiage, he didn't dare give the only pertinent answer:

"You don't know what you're talking about. These are things you'll never understand at all."

What good would it do to try to explain that Tamara was the in-carnation of the lady in courtly romances, the one who surrounds everything that comes near her with an aura of beauty and purity, the one for the love of whom one is ready to endure a thousand trials, and who gives her hand only to the man who has been able to dream of her with the greatest constancy?

September soon came. The vacation was already almost over when one morning Ariane, to whom the postman had just delivered a large package, came, smiling slyly, to find him in his room.

"This seems to be for you, my dear. Once again, I'm only the inter-mediary," she added as she handed him a strange missive.

It was by its scent that he recognized it. That violet perfume! It had been a long time since he'd smelled it. But he hadn't yet for-gotten it, no. And then the envelope, square in shape. And the pale green ink, whose like he'd never seen . . . He couldn't read the let-ter without feeling himself blush. It was taking him back, with the abruptness of the unexpected, to a past that seemed to him so dis-tant. More than a year had gone by since he'd had any direct word from Violetta. And here she was back again. There was not, this time, a single verse in her letter. Violetta, who had remained intermittently in touch with Ariane, had slipped, into the book she was sending to her friend as a birthday present, a message for Manuel, whom she didn't know how to contact. She wanted to inform him that after spending a year in the United States, she'd now settled for a time in Paris. She spoke of a "fiancé" she'd had over there, one of her young professors at the university, who had greatly disappointed her. She'd had to leave him, not without a scene, after several months of living together, just before the planned marriage. She definitely preferred France. She asked him how he was doing. How he was experiencing the Parisian dream he'd so often talked to her about. And, finally, she suggested that he get in touch with her, when he had a chance, so that they could catch up on things, as they'd promised to do.

Embarrassed, he replied evasively to Ariane's questions, which surprised her. As soon as she'd left, he slipped Violetta's letter into a corner of his suitcase, taking care not to mix it with the package that contained Tamara's letters. He promised himself that he would pay no attention to the intruder.

12

Second Start

Still another vestige, reader, of my old attempts to write a novel! Hard not to see that, isn't it? However, it's much later than the preceding ones. End of the 1960s, this time (the year of Our Lord 1969, to be precise): the period when I made a fleeting return to my old literary dogmas. I'd once again yielded here, as in the very first chapter, to what I might call, a little grandiloquently, the demon of alteration. Which led me, once again, to make things seem much worse than they were. At the expense of the truth, of course.

My unfortunate hero, instead of tranquilly enjoying the pleasures of returning to his native country – well earned pleasures, you'll have to agree, given the difficult year he'd just been through – saw, on the contrary, by my decision alone, his uneasiness growing and getting more serious. A decision that was, however, not entirely unjustified. In fact, in the vast project of a *Bildungsroman* from which I'd abstained during the whole period of the 1968 rebellion, but that, immediately afterward, I'd started thinking about again, I had to take my Manuel all the way to a double failure. First, I had to confront him directly with his inability to act on his own history. Second, I had to make him realize the extent of the rupture, increasingly difficult to surmount, with his whole entourage. These failures were required by critical realism. No question of evading them . . .

Reality, once stripped of my retrospective alterations, was far less dramatic. After a summer that had been, on the whole, rather pleasant, the beginning of my second school year in Paris, in khâgne this time, took place without any melancholy, and even with a certain good humor. No resemblance to the preceding year. Passing through, on 30 September, at five in the afternoon (it was raining, of course, that fine drizzle that always falls on such occasions), the door on the Rue Saint-Jacques, I had, as strange as it might seem, a feeling that I was coming home. I hardly noticed the iron grillwork that was one day so greatly to intimidate my freshly arrived hero and interpose itself between his eyes and the external world; on that day, it seemed an innocuous stage prop.

I rejoined with pleasure most of my classmates, in particular those whom the events of June had brought closer to me: the Algerian war occupied a more and more prominent place in our conversations. Others, who had not been able to gain admission to khâgne, sent me notes asking me not to forget our common commitments. I was flattered, and vowed to see them again as soon as I could. But above all, I was surprised to find, in the mail waiting for me in the concierge's booth, a message from Fabrice, the only one I'd had since he'd left.

He was somewhat disappointed, the intrepid traveler, and not displeased to be re-entering the fold. Even prepared to re-enter khâgne with his pals, since the Strass (the administration), in its mercy, was willing to take him back, despite his escapade! After his months of wandering in the tropics, he'd brought back, he said, only one bit of booty: a few very heart-felt pages on the sadness and uselessness of such journeys. I only half believed him, sure that he was greatly exaggerating his disillusionment and that he would leave again at the first opportunity. But what a joy it would be to see him again! He was one of the few privileged people whose errors I was prepared, I don't know why, to accept as excusable, whose privileges I was prepared to accept as legitimate. And then, he'd had some responsibility for what had happened to me. He alone had launched me, by giving me Sonia's letter, into my great adventure. I was going to be able to tell him what had happened afterward. He would certainly be surprised by the turn things had taken. Maybe he'd even be able to get me going. He knew what to do, and he had experience with women!

So everything looked good, so far as my friends were concerned. The main thing, of course, remained: Tamara. The letters and cards we'd exchanged during the summer, in a regular rhythm that reassured me and made Ariane smile, had left me partly unsatisfied. For (on this point, at least, the transposition into a novel hardly altered the facts) love, which was supposed to have been their single

99

theme, the irreplaceable and omnipresent substance, had been the great unmentioned. The situation had to be set right as soon as possible, an end put to ambiguity, so that the joy of my return might be at least as great as the trial of separation. But as a result of various conflicting commitments, and despite all my efforts, three weeks later I still had not been able to re-establish direct contact with my friend.

I'd never ceased, during all this time, to plan the order of what was soon going to be the evening of our reunion. Our first rendezvous since the party! Of course, what I would have liked was a party exactly like the other one, or better yet, the same party, miraculously prolonged, which would have erased at a single stroke all those months we had spent apart. But where could such a miracle be achieved? Our favorite brasserie, the Lido? No, it wasn't equal to the importance of the event. I finally decided on an elegant restaurant located at the very bottom of the Rue Saint-Jacques, whose praises Fabrice had sung: "An intimate setting, Bach or Mozart in the background, impeccable and discreet service, everything you need, in short." He'd taken several of his own girlfriends there, "with complete success!" he'd added, to reassure me. I would have reserved in advance a table for two, off by itself, in the upper corner of the terrace, from which the towers of Notre-Dame could be seen. I was sure that this tête-à-tête would suffice to eliminate all doubts. I'd look at Tamara in a way that would make her fully aware of what I was feeling, and her eyes would be able to give me an almost simultaneous reply. This simple exchange would abolish in an instant all the distances between us, and I already saw, immediately afterward, the sweet, slow movements of her arms going around me, while I would run my hands through her hair. But when I was finally able to reach her on the telephone, and we were able to arrange a rendezvous, there was no question of dinner. After considerable hesitation, a decision was made: a simple evening at the Odéon. The three of us. With Sonia. "It's like before!" they said to me in unison when we met at the entrance to the theater. I pretended to be overjoyed. However, nothing could have shown me more clearly that between my friend and me, everything had to begin all over again.

13
Suspicion

Autumn 1958

Between Tamara and Manuel, everything had to begin all over again. But in a very different context. For him, as for his two friends, a great many new obligations had arisen along with the new school year. Having received their baccalaureates, they were now both studying at the university. Sonia had enthusiastically begun studying architecture. Tamara had finally decided on art history. They no longer had as much time of their own on Saturdays and Sundays. So the wonderful regularity of the preceding spring was over. How often they would be able to go out as a threesome remained for some time uncertain. Subject, in fact, to the whims of Sonia, to whom Manuel and Tamara left it to direct things, as they had the year before.

She'd gotten it into her head to make them share her passion for certain unusual aspects of the Parisian architectural landscape. She haughtily disregarded what she called the funereal quarters, the faubourg Saint-Germain and its townhouses, which she found even more sinister than the arrogant old men who had earlier lived in them, and she described with disgust, as if she had herself been imprisoned in them, the succession of dark rooms, full of taciturn portraits, long-silent pianos, and grandfather clocks black with dirt. Her rage grew even greater when she spoke of what she called the monuments for idiotic tourists. She would gladly have razed Saint-Sulpice's towers and the Panthéon's cupola. Even Notre-Dame was redeemed in her eyes only for very special reasons. If she agreed one day to accompany Tamara and Manuel there (not without having made a detour to see the statue of Étienne Dolet in the Place Maubert), it was not merely, as she hastened to tell them, because of her interest in Gothic architecture. And she began to speak, in a hushed

voice, of the role the cathedral had played as an assembly point for
the people of Paris, mentioning the processions, the fêtes, the ker-
mises, and the countless games in which Parisians' energy found an
outlet, apart from any religious concern.

Her taste thus took them, with increasing frequency, toward old,
popular Paris: the artisans' workshops around the Bastille, narrow
and deep, that could hardly be glimpsed through their dusty windows; second-hand shops shamelessly overflowing onto the side-
walks in order to display the kind of bric-a-brac that delighted Manuel during his lonely walks around the flea market. Always on the
lookout for vestiges of the past, Sonia sometimes stopped in front
of the gray, imposing façade of an empty building that had been
abandoned for decades, in order to discover, with an emotion she
would have liked to transmit to them, that it was ("can you believe
that!") a former tramway depot ("which should be restored someday, after all, don't you think?"). Or else there were long pauses in
the midst of a demolition site (a great deal of demolishing was then
being done in all those neighborhoods, and not always with discernment). Between two windowless façades, behind fences covered with
posters and graffiti, they cautiously slipped, in single file, among
the mounds of cast-off beams and doors, pipes and washbasins, in
order to contemplate sections of walls that stood there, completely
naked, and on which their very recent past could still be read. She
tried to make them see the traces of the different floors – "a real
stratigraphic section, isn't it?" – with the marks of floors and ceil-
ings, the panels of wallpaper on which one could see the shapes of
the furniture and the pictures that had, for generations, been up
against them. One Sunday, she even went so far as to take them, in
the freezing rain, on a long pilgrimage to the Père Lachaise cemetery,
where she absolutely insisted on seeing Abelard's tomb.

Manuel didn't care much for these new activities. He was convinced they were disturbing his relationship with Tamara. Worse
yet, they were threatening to poison it, or even put an end to it.
Why were his friend's messages no longer arriving, as they had before, exactly on the day they were expected? Why were rendezvous
planned long in advance and duly confirmed canceled by a *pneu-*

matique that offered few explanations? This reawakened in him old worries, the ones he'd thought, since the pact sealed in the Tuileries, definitively eliminated. At such moments, everything seemed to him up in the air again: the tiny steps forward he was trying to make, every time they went out together, along the path toward renewed closeness to Tamara, and that he thought had been taken, now seemed to him to have been unexpectedly erased. As if everything that came from her now constituted only a fragile gift, one that could be revoked at any time. And this went on at least until their next outing.

The worst thing was that he felt more and more often that he didn't understand the situation at all. He couldn't help noticing a contrast between the content of the increasingly infrequent letters he received directly from Tamara, which were almost all imbued with affection—an affection that was discreet, to be sure, but in his view, at least, clearly perceptible—and that of their conversations as a threesome on Sundays. Now, they all seemed to be watching what they said. Despite the efforts of Sonia, who made provocative quips from time to time, the conversation remained conventional, limited to exchanging general, tasteful remarks on the play or film currently in fashion. To the point that sometimes, almost as soon as a meeting he'd found "lukewarm," "listless," or "really disappointing" (that was the way he characterized them in the evening, when he wrote them down in his little black notebook) was over, he felt a violent need to reread some of her old letters. To reassure himself. But soon, not even this calmed him.

What pained him was that these variations and these contrasts seemed to him arbitrary, foreign to any logic. "It's a question of female moods," he told himself as a consolation, from the height of his male vanity, which had come galloping back for the occasion. Or else he hastened to put it down to the attacks of modesty that must overcome Tamara when they met as a threesome. Doubt crept in nonetheless. There were even moments when, annoyed, he began to suspect the worst kind of trickery. "What if she's giving somebody else, someone bolder, what I don't dare take, or even ask for?" This idea tormented him. He couldn't think back without fury on his first disappointment in love: the discovery, in the course of his fourteenth year, that women were changeable. He owed this discovery to his friend Luce. Despite Ariane's reticence, they had openly "gone together" for at least three months, leaving the middle school together, going to the movies or the theater together. Then came the summer vacation, which separated them. He awaited the end of the vacation with impatience. On the first day of school, Luce arrived arm in arm with Antoine, the very boy whom they had both labeled, by common agreement, as the most vulgar in the class ... So now, when in the course of an outing as a threesome they met one of Tamara's friends, he watched the way they looked at each other, tried to follow the succession of laughs and smiles on their faces and decipher its meaning. When these friends were young men he suspected of being rivals, he betrayed an ill humor on the verge of turning into hatred. At those moments, with the somewhat obstinate pride that in him took the place of energy, he felt far more capable of bruising than of caressing. Then he learned to conceal better the intensity of his fears, and adopted, when confronted by a third person, an air of indifference or superficiality.

Sometimes, however, he succeeded in forgetting his jealousy. But only to give free rein to the fantasies that were coursing through him. In his mad desire for an explanation of Tamara's attitude, some evenings he went so far as to seek it (contrary to his declared convictions) in her Russian origins, and to that end rounded up commonplaces and clichés. "Ah, Tamara, Tamara," he was to write one day, "no doubt there is still something in you of those Muscovite girls of the last century. They were capable, it was said, of kissing with amorous enthusiasm a portrait of a grand duke, and of taking, in those pasteboard kisses, an inexpressible pleasure. But they were hardly available, afterward, for other effusions ... Unless in your case it's a remnant of that severity even your Dostoevsky considers inseparable from the Russian soul. Oh, yes, you're amusing yourself, you cruel thing, by treating me like a toy. And in doing so, you're repeating the atavistic reflexes of a lord dealing with his muzhiks ..."

Or else he fell back on other, still more misplaced stereotypes. He looked up in his readings all the examples of the "Belle Dame sans Merci"[40] he could, identifying himself, of course, with the suffering lover. Then he felt a bitter pride in having found, for his first passion, so perfect an incarnation of the femme fatale . . .

Such were, in his hour of doubt, his ravings, whose very excess soon deflated them. Then Manuel returned to his usual feelings, and, far from accusing his friend, sought excuses for her, which he had no difficulty in finding. She was entirely right in not making a greater commitment to him! She must have sensed that his passion for her was not yet sufficiently pure, not yet absolute enough to eliminate all the rest, all the dross he was ashamed of. Yes, he had remained at bottom, in spite of himself, sensitive to other emotions, ready to yield to other promptings. He regretted his multiple little love affairs over the summer, to which he had not been able to avoid making some very vague, very evasive allusions. He was angry with himself for having in this way perhaps wounded his friend's sensibility, aroused her distrust. How could she have known that everything he did away from her was for him a mere trifle that had nothing in common with his love for her?

Thus he retained, from one outing to the next, a taste of melancholy at the heart of what would have counted, the preceding year, as one of his moments of happiness. And sometimes even the bursts of joy, of gaiety, and of delight that filled him when he was near her suddenly dissipated, giving way to an oppressive, persistent inertia that interfered with the progress of his schoolwork. He no longer knew how he should behave.

He hesitated to talk about all this to Fabrice, with whom he quite often ate lunch, as he had the preceding year. He'd already told him, when they'd met again at the beginning of the school year, a large part of the story. He'd even shown him a few of the things he'd written, at least those that, despite his constant fear of being discovered, he hadn't had the heart to destroy and that he hid at the bottom of his lockers.

"Well, at least you've not forgotten the art of Petrarchizing, it seems! Go on, then, since it seems to amuse you. *Trahit sua quemque*[41] . . . But anyway, we'll see where you are in a few weeks, so far as *voluptas* is concerned," Fabrice had said to him.

As encouragement, it wasn't much. Disappointed, but retaining all his confidence in his friend's perspicacity, he told himself that Fabrice would no doubt understand matters much better if he knew Tamara, if he saw her, if he spoke with her. So he proposed, a few days later, that Fabrice accompany them to a performance of *The Persians* in the Sorbonne's main amphitheater, which was to be put on by the Ancient Theater group. Sonia couldn't go, and her seat was available. Fabrice grumbled at first.

"Museum theater, pseudo-archaeological reconstitutions, all that, as you are well aware, bores me to tears. I'm not like you. I like living theater!"

He went along all the same. But during the conversation that followed the performance, he and Tamara didn't hit it off at all. She found him cold and mocking, much too inclined to take pleasure in the negative side of things.

"It's so easy, you understand, to make fun of everything, to show the falsity of everything!" she'd said, coming alive as soon as Fabrice had left them (abruptly, as he always did). "He can't do anything but denounce, denounce, denounce. Well, I, you see, I like people to be able to celebrate, yes, to cel-e-brate, from time to time!"

As for Fabrice, his verdict on Tamara was delivered the following day.

"Perfect, my friend, perfect. And even more than perfect. Body and soul, as somebody said. A real Virgin. But in my opinion, there's something bothering her somewhere. Around her halo, maybe. It must pinch a bit... If I were in your place? Well, precisely, I'm not in it, and I'd never have gotten myself into it, either. Virgins – I leave 'em in their niches, somewhere at the back of the altar. If necessary, in museums. But nowhere else, no, nowhere!"

Manuel was rather ashamed, therefore, after all that, to try again. But he did so anyway. Who else could be his confidant?

"Old pal, this scenario isn't familiar to me, you already know that," Fabrice began by saying. "For this type of girl, I have no user's manual."

A pause.

"That said, if you really think I can help get things going . . . Do you want me to be your ambassador to your Madonna? To tell her that for more than a year her lovely eyes have been killing you with love, but that you haven't yet found the right way to tell her about it? For after all, that's what it's really about, isn't it? You don't want me to? Really don't? Well, all right, I won't insist . . . But then what?"

Another pause.

"Look, why don't we approach by a carom, so to speak? Yes, as in billiards. Well, what do you say? A nice little get-together between me and the pseudo-sister. She wrote me, a long time ago, didn't she? That was what started this whole thing. It's high time I answered her letter. Courtesy! Elementary courtesy, my dear Watson. She claimed to admire my rantings, at the time. She couldn't refuse to give me, after all, just between the two of us, a few little hints about the state of the charming cousin's heart. And maybe also about that of her loins . . . Loins are important in these things, don't you think? And why not her liver, and her spleen, and the rest . . . That would allow you to find out what to expect in the whole organism of your Dulcinea . . . That would be a big step forward for you, wouldn't it?"

That much offhandedness scandalized Manuel. This spoiled child's skepticism! This perpetual sarcasm of the successful! For the first time since he'd known him, Manuel brusquely interrupted his friend. He was sorry he'd appealed to him. He now saw that Fabrice, despite all his amorous conquests, or perhaps because of them, knew nothing about love. That far from helping him, he was capable of ruining everything. He thanked him coldly. Asked him to keep out of all this, for the time being. Later on, maybe, he added, insincerely.

He felt alone again. So he turned to his ultimate recourse, books: what could they tell him about his love, about the behavior to adopt in a situation like his? After a few weeks, he took stock of what he'd learned.

March 59

So you buried yourself in your books again. That's no surprise! They've always been your best interlocutors. But what a sinuous path to arrive at your present conclusions! You didn't bother to re-read the great classics. You've already seen that the idyllic world that made you dream so much is not the one you live in. So you went to works dealing with sexuality, eroticism (are they the same thing?), since that's what obsesses you. You entered there a domain that your more than puritanical education had neglected, and that only Violetta's lessons, and the practical exercise that accompanied them, had helped you cultivate.

Your first incursions brought you a few surprises. You had in your hands, last week, an old edition, bound in red and decorated with engravings of an anatomical realism such as you've never seen before, of the Philosophy in the Boudoir[42] (it was a nonresident student named Castelair, an odd bird, to tell the truth, who had circulated this book in a hardly clandestine manner). You don't understand the craze for this book, and for a few others by the same dismal author, at the Lycée. You opened it with curiosity. You expected to succumb, as Fabrice had said you would, to a dizzying experience: a book that fearlessly goes, in matters of thought as well as of sex, to the boldest extremes! The nec plus ultra! But, from your first contact with it, the ponderous, pedantic, and tiresome sermons on pleasure, which form the backbone of the divine marquis's philosophy, put you off. As for the sexual practices minutely described for pages and pages, they seemed to you to have more to do with the circus than with love. Lacking any evocative power, they made no more impression on you, when you managed to get through them, than the constructions you made as a child with your erector set. How can one take all that seriously, even for a minute? There's something there that escapes you. In any case, there's nothing for you to learn from this muck-up (you don't dare write: fuck-up). Is it worthwhile to go plunge, in order to decontaminate yourself, into Restif de La Bretonne's Anti-Justine, where, dixit Fabrice, love is presented in a less sinister light? Probably not . . .

Then you moved on to a new series of works, this time more composite. A few of them, attributed to authors you didn't expect to find there, Stendhal, Apollinaire, Malraux, Aragon . . . But on reading these texts, you couldn't help feeling embarrassed. Whether by the outrageous aspect of the language, whose puerile rawness too often spills over into gross farce, or, on the contrary, by the contrast between a polished, even occasionally shimmering style, and the systematically scabrous nature of the scenes described. What interest is there in that? The others, openly "zobscene" (as people say here) books or magazines of the kind easily found on the quays of the Seine, no longer have anything to do with either love or literature. The tedious monotony of all that! To think that at the same time, it is drummed into us, at the rate of six hours a week, that Eros is nothing but the human desire to transcend the limits of human existence, the limits imposed on us by time and space, in order to arrive at a synoptic view of Being [sic], or else that love is a sacred rite providing access to the Absolute [re-sic!].

So you turned your curiosity elsewhere. By accident, you recently came across, at the PUF bookstore on the Boul'Mich, a collection of articles under the title Psychoanalysis and Biology. Why did you buy it, why did you begin reading it, when you have no particular interest in either biology or psychoanalysis, about which, in truth, you knew almost nothing? More than by the title, your curiosity was awakened by the author's name: Marie Bonaparte. No less... The appearance of this patronymic, which you didn't expect in such a context, immediately elicited in your mind the idea of a secret family relationship between Napoleon and Freud, an idea you couldn't help finding comical, and seductive. It's through this work that you've become familiar with a few scraps of Freudian theory. Desire, the libido, etc. You felt finally understood, and absolved. For up to that point, admit it, you weren't entirely certain that you were not, at least a little, guilty. Should you give this book (or another of the same school) to Tamara? She would certainly learn a great deal from it! But she's probably not ready for that. Later, maybe.

As a result, he was no longer afraid to blithely mix his love and his desire, the intensity of the one being identified, for him, with the violence of the other. He would no longer be satisfied with a nameless desire or a speechless love. His past resistance and prudence were transformed into spurs. As if the only result of this long postponement of the declaration had been to exasperate his amorous appetite.

It was then that the memory of Violetta, once again, forced itself on him. Manuel rediscovered – not without difficulty, because since the preceding summer it had lain forgotten in a side pocket of his suitcase – the letter in which she gave him her address. He sent her a note. Intentionally short and anodyne. By a pneumatique that was just as brief, she invited him to lunch the following Sunday. He decided to accept. What was he risking? Now that he felt justified in his love and in his desire, why should he stay away from a girl who had been such an agreeable accomplice, and who could become a friend? He even persuaded himself that it would be to his advantage to cultivate this friendship openly. Maybe he would succeed, in this way, in arousing in Tamara a spurt of concern, or even – who knew? – of jealousy, which would make her overcome her reserve.

14

Violetta Revisited

Here I explain for your benefit, friendly reader, that the novel of the 1960s of which you have just read another chapter, adhered rather strictly to reality. At least reality as I remember it. Yes, Tamara's distancing, Manuel's suspicions and torments, Fabrice's disappointing casualness, the consolation sought and finally found in books – none of that was invented. Not even the virtuous annoyance with Sade's sudden success . . .

As for the rest of the story, things are still clearer. I'll simply let you read my notes, which are approximately contemporary with the events reported.

22 March 59

So you've seen her again, your old Violetta. But things between you are taking a strange turn. Completely unexpected. Indeed, one might even say that the situation is getting complicated. And all that in one week. Got to get clear about this. Let's review.

Act I

As promised, you went to her place last Sunday. She lives in an out-of-the-way part of the fourteenth arrondissement, near the Plaisance metro station. To you, who had never yet set foot beyond Port-Royal (except on that day when, with Tamara and Sonia, you found the entrance to the Catacombs closed), it seemed like the other end of the world. By asking for directions twice after coming out of the metro, you finally found yourself at the end of a strange dead-end street that was completely invisible from outside it. A series of small, low buildings, in front of which a few little gardens are barely staying alive. In one of these buildings, Violetta occupies a studio on the ground floor, which you find rather dark. Moreover, it's dusty and full of books. You didn't expect a boudoir hung with velvet, cashmere, and silk, of course, but the simplicity of the decoration surprises you. Almost no furni-

ture, except, in a sort of alcove, a low double bed, with a Berber blanket with geometrical motifs (no other visible trace of her year in Morocco) serving as a bedspread.

Physically, Violetta has changed. More adult, even more a woman than she had been back in Morocco, which is saying quite a bit! The long black hair is still there, even blacker and more opulent, perhaps, than you remembered it. Her eyes and mouth are rather heavily made up: you recognize immediately the carmine lipstick that she was already wearing (it had a little sugary taste full of charm). And of course the delicious little breasts, firm and high, which remain noticeable under her tight blouse (did she do it on purpose?).

Somewhat awkward at first. You don't know how to act, especially when she begins to compliment you, as she used to do, on your physique: should you take these compliments seriously? She served you a little glass of Beaujolais, quickly set the table, and you immediately sat down to eat. The meal was very simple (salad, rare ground beef, spaghetti with butter on it): Violetta claims to have no interest in cooking, or in housekeeping in general. But the wine and the camembert have a taste that you won't forget. In bits and pieces, amid exclamations and interruptions, which become increasingly frequent as the meal goes on, each of you tells the other what has happened since your steamy days in Morocco. She refused to dwell on her American misadventure.

"A mistake . . . Inexcusable . . . The next time, take my word for it, I'll think twice before I promise to marry a man. Anyway, to tell the truth, I have no desire, really none at all any more, to get married."

For your part, encouraged by her questions, after a few hesitations, you talked about Tamara. About your love. About the dead-end at which you've arrived.

"That doesn't surprise me. You had that kind of affair coming to you."

And when you tried to protest, she went on:

"Yes, you did! You know it! Your eternal timidity, your attacks of purely verbal boldness, your regrets! I know you. In fact, there's nothing you like better than waiting. And hoping, of course. Back there, already, if I hadn't taken things into my own hands . . ."

A pause.

"Anyway, it's not entirely your fault, no doubt. This must be a matter of education. Or maybe heredity, who knows?"

She wished you good luck despite everything, and even admitted, with a strange smile, that she wouldn't mind being loved like that someday.

"But don't worry, there's no hurry. I've got lots of time. There are much more urgent things in my life!"

And you laughed, laughed freely, seeing how much, in less than two years, your paths had diverged, and yet how much pleasure you found in being together again. You promised each other, at the end, not to go months and months before seeing each other.

You went home satisfied and worried at the same time: would this renewed contact with Violetta really help you in your relationship with Tamara? Come on, now! Don't delude yourself too much! Strategy·in love has never been your strong point.

Act II

Last Saturday (that is, yesterday), Sonia and Tamara once again canceled at the last minute. Without even giving any reason . . . So it seemed to you completely natural to call Violetta right away. To invite her to dinner. You owed her that much, for sure! She seemed surprised to hear from you.

"That's nice of you. But this evening, I can't. I'm going to invite some friends over for a little drink. A little party, completely on the spur of the moment."

A pause.

"That said, you're welcome, if you want to come. Yes, come then, it'll give you a change from your eternal khâgneux. Come on, I insist."

You accepted. Because you couldn't bear the idea of spending still another Saturday night alone at the movies, as you did back in the bad old days. But also, admit it, because you were curious to see what it might be like, a party with people of the same kind as Violetta. Up to that point, she still had in your eyes something strange and unique. You remembered above all the lone she-wolf. So you were happy to be able to go back to her place as an observer. Better yet, as an explorer. A sort of ethnological expedition, in short. And one that might not be useless for you, at this stage.

You weren't disappointed. When you got there, at least fifteen people, the majority of them girls, it seemed to you, were jammed into the studio, which a very small lamp with a violet-colored shade lit dimly. People of all ages, none of whom seemed to be over thirty, except a tall, bearded man with a stentorian voice who was leaning against a wall. Two couples, their lips glued to each other and their bodies interlaced, forming two almost immobile blocks, pretended to be dancing to a blues song. The other guests, for the most part sitting on the floor, were drinking gin or vodka, smoking, kissing each other, caressing each other more or less discreetly, or else following the music, humming or tapping their fingers in accord with the rhythm. A sort of sweet intimacy seemed to bind together everyone present.

"Make way for the young people! A little room for our surprise guest . . ."

Very maternally, Violetta sat you down between Chantal and Francine, who were sitting on a corner of the bed.

"An old accomplice I'd lost, but fortunately found again . . . Yes. My glorious African campaign. Not too bad, huh?"

It was in these terms that she introduced you, laughing, to your two neighbors.

"He doesn't know anyone here. Take care of him for a while, you two. I'm counting on you."

They rapidly sized you up before giving you, in unison, their most radiant smiles. The welcome was certainly exquisite, and you began to feel confident. Nonetheless, you didn't try to take part, except by brief remarks on details, in the three or four conversations that were going on simultaneously, and to which you tried to lend an ear in turns. You limited yourself to listening, picking up along the way a few names (Borges, Gramsci, Pavese, Antonioni, Moreno, Bataille) and a few words or expressions that seemed to recur the most often in one or another of the conversations: phantasm, transgression, dogmatism, psychodrama, pushing the limits of enjoyment. You were not really able to understand what the various interlocutors were driving at. Except when the tall bearded man, imposing silence on everyone, began to make a speech, or rather to prophesy. He heralded the impending flood of Eros that was going to overwhelm Western civilization. "Yes," he repeated, "the obsession with love, desire, and enjoyment are going to become the major ingredients in the play of supply and demand." The others unanimously nodded in agreement.

When, shortly after midnight, you looked like you were getting ready to leave, Violetta protested.

"What? Already? The two of us have hardly seen each other. Stay a little longer. There's no hurry, after all . . ."

You didn't dare remind her, in front of everyone, that you were supposed to be back in the Lycée before one a.m. She sat down very close to you for a moment. Right up against you, rather. As she used to down back in Morocco. Laughing very hard, she poured you a glass of gin.

"Come on, swallow that, my fine friend, you can use it."

You laughed, and forcing yourself, drank. You would have preferred vodka, but the only bottle had long since been drained by the bearded man and his ebullient followers. You danced a little, cheek to cheek, with the blond Chantal, who left you rather quickly saying that she had to go to another party, which was supposed to last until dawn, way out in the twentieth arrondissement. Then you turned to Francine. She didn't feel like dancing. So you talked, despite the noise. She'd also done a year of preparatory study last year. At the Lycée Fénélon. But she'd dropped out before the end of the year, disgusted. She'd enrolled at the Sorbonne. At first in sociology, because of Gurvitch. She loved his grating accent: exactly like her grandfather's! A few weeks ago, she'd also begun studying linguistics. She adores it. "It's the science of the future," she keeps repeating. You agreed with her wholeheartedly, hardly having to feign conviction, so much did you want to please her. She gave you a look of gratitude. As she left you, and without your having spoken up to that point of seeing each other again, she delicately slipped into the hip pocket of your velvet pants a matchbox on whose back she had scribbled her telephone number. A nice little apartment within a stone's throw of the Bastille: she shares it with her friend Céline, who's hardly ever there, moreover . . .

"Above all, don't hesitate. But never in the morning, please! See you soon, then . . . Why not next Saturday, if you're free? You'll let me know, okay?"

"Yes, of course, I'll let you know . . ." (and without knowing quite why, you kissed her on the neck, just long enough to smell the acid odor of her sweat).

It was after two a.m. Almost all at the same time, the other guests also decided to leave. You were the only one left, and you were getting ready to take off as well. Violetta, who had already begun picking up the empty bottles and full ashtrays, started laughing.

"Come on, now, you know it's too late to go back to your prestigious school, Monsieur le Khâgneux. However, don't worry, my dear, you're not going to have to spend the night outside. You're much too delicate!"

You said nothing, thought nothing, except that you'd let yourself be cornered, once again. For a moment, you saw only a great void before you. Then, as if moved by a reflex, despite the gin (or rather because of it) you resorted to one of the things you used to do back in Morocco. You drew Violetta toward you and took her in your arms, happy to feel against your chest the warmth of those breasts you'd so much liked to play with. Without pulling away, on the contrary, with her eyes half-closed, she nodded, smiling, and ran her hands again and again through the curls of your hair. Slowly, with a slight back-and-forth movement and an infinite gentleness. As she knew so well how to do back in Morocco, on the sofa in the living room. Then she put her mouth delicately on yours. And you immediately rediscovered, arising from the contact with her moist and slightly sugary lips, from her agile tongue, the flavor, identical in every way, of your kisses back there. As if some secret shortcut had suddenly pulled you away from the normal flow of time in order to send you into a parallel flow, where nothing any longer separates you from those past moments: on the red wool carpet, you're both stretched out, not yet entirely naked, your limbs closely interlaced, moving gently and already sweating slightly, Albinoni's music hardly discernible in the background, the dark velvet curtains drawn, and outside it's hot, so hot, that you feel you're going to melt, simply melt. The night, the alcohol, and the memory so abruptly resuscitated soon erased whatever distance still remained between you and Violetta. And, for just an instant, you thought your truth was really there, in this body-to-body contact finally found again with your expert former accomplice, that everything else, this new self that you'd laboriously constructed since your arrival here, was only a pointless and fastidious detour.

It was only this morning that you came to, and realized what had happened. Violetta was already up, and, wearing only a tiny pair of black lace panties, was keeping an eye on the pot she'd put on her old electric hotplate, which was emitting a reddish glow. You'd hardly opened your eyes when she gave you what was meant to be a friendly greeting.

"Ah, there's something I'm finally going to be able to tell to you, Manuel, and that will certainly interest you: you're even cuter when you're sleeping. Just like a baby, I swear! I've been admiring the sight for a good quarter of an hour."

Not very cheery, you looked around the room to orient yourself. At the foot of the bed, mixed-up clothes: a wrinkled white shirt, a long black skirt, a rather rumpled pair of velvet pants. Scattered on the floor, the contents of your pockets. A few coins. A box of matches. And especially keys, the keys to your precious lockers, the ones in which you kept the records of your correspondence with Tamara. How did all that get there? A mystery. Your surprise and embarrassment must have been so obvious that they made Violetta laugh.

"Ah, naturally, everything happened in a certain disorder . . . whence this sight, which seems to pain you. Of course, it had nothing in common with the way we used to undress each other. Do you remember? Just on my garter alone, the time you could spend! Not to mention my bra. But you seemed to be in such a hurry, all of a sudden! Come, come, don't be like that, for heaven's sake. You didn't do anything wrong, I assure you. On the contrary, even, if you'd like to know the whole truth . . . What do you expect, as someone said, two bodies never forget each other. Especially when they've known each other so intimately, right? And then, you recall, we hadn't entirely settled our accounts: you owed me a real night, and even, if I remember correctly, a mad night. As for me, I owed you . . . I owed you what you jumped on as soon as everyone left. It must have been pretty urgent! My poor love, you've been deprived so long . . . Well, anyway, now we're even on that score, let's say no more about it. We can gaily start out on a new basis . . . No, no, please don't give me that scared look. I have no intention of sinking my hooks into you, my handsome one! If it'll reassure you, we'll say that our new pact will be the same as the one back there. After all, that worked pretty well, didn't it? You remember: no sentimental nonsense. To which I would only add: no untimely jealousy. So you can keep her as long as you want, your Dulcinea from the Volga. I don't think she'll bother us much. We could even go out together, arm in arm. If I correctly understood what you told me the other day, you're used to threesomes, aren't you? Yes, I know, it shocks you when I talk that way. But what do you expect? What else can I do with you? You're one of those dreamers who think that there's a big difference between the love one feels and the love one makes. But just between you and me, I think that in three months you'll have gotten tired, and given up . . . Something else that has nothing to do with this: not too much nonsense with Francine, please. She's a real friend, and she's extremely fragile. She gets infatuated very quickly. She might get ideas, I'm sure she's already gotten some, and be very unhappy afterward. So be careful! There, I'm going to end up doing *everything for you, handsome. I've put the final touches on my role as initiator, tomorrow I can start my role as . . . call it what you will. It's up to you, my sweet!*

You listened to this terrible speech without turning a hair. What could you say? You quickly got dressed. You claimed you had to finish a philosophy essay as soon as possible. In order to make this more plausible, you even specified the subject: "The courage to think." And you took off for the Lycée, where you were unable to do anything except hastily write these notes. All this came all by itself. Everything is still fresh in your head. Because of your indignation, which refuses to go away.

So that's where you are for the moment. And of course, you don't know what to do.

Act III

You'd like to be able to write: there will be no Act III. But how can one know, with someone as unpredictable as you?

15

Louvre

There was no Act III.

Well, let's say, almost none. In any case, not right away.

A very violent attack of remorse, accompanied by an equally violent disgust with myself, kept me out of Violetta's bed for several weeks. No, it was certainly not for that denouement, no matter how pleasant it might be (and God knows, it *was* pleasant!) that my heart had beaten so much, for so many months! And I felt more disposed to welcome the sorrows that would come to me from Tamara than all the pleasures given by others.

During these weeks, in the conversations I had with Violetta – for I couldn't keep from calling her sometimes and even seeing her briefly in her favorite little bar in the Rue de Plaisance – she didn't spare me her sarcasm.

"You remember what our dear old Baudelaire said: Enivrez-vous?[43] Well, you two could always get drunk . . . on chastity! I can see from here the picture you'd make, you and your vestal. A full color image! Or rather not. A real monochrome, two white swans embracing on a glacier . . . And to set it all off, a little background of lilies and dove's feathers. It'd be better than Alphonse Allais!"

I accepted all this sarcasm calmly.

That was because in the meantime, a new turnaround had occurred. Just when I was beginning to despair, my meetings with Tamara had started up again, with such intensity that I no longer had much occasion, or desire, to look elsewhere. She had simply imagined that I might be able to help her in her work, to give her the benefit, as she put it, of my "experience." Although secretly very skeptical regarding the interest of the aforementioned experience, I had leapt at the opportunity. My role was going to consist chiefly of accompanying my friend, as often as possible, to the Louvre, for she wanted, she said, to bury herself in it with me "to explore it in depth." The noble gray edifice, with its labyrinth of rooms and galleries, thus became the refuge of our Sunday escapades, in which Sonia had declined from the outset to participate.

I remembered with embarrassment the first visits I'd made to the Louvre the preceding year, just a few days after my arrival in Paris. Ashamed of my inability to tell an amphora from a crater, a copperplate engraving from a dry-point, a Boucher from a Boudin, I had thought it useful to join, one Thursday afternoon, a group of middle-school students being led around by an old, red-haired guide, a tall skinny fellow who constantly flailed his arms about like a mad windmill. I trotted through several galleries with them. Without seeing anything, without understanding anything, without feeling anything. It was such a new world, the one I bumped into that day! A world that seemed to me to be composed essentially of goddesses and martyrs, male and female saints, but also and especially *Annunciations* and *Adorations*, *Crucifixions* and *Depositions*, *Transfigurations* and *Lamentations*. This made me feel so uncomfortable that I'd vowed never to go back there except when I was alone, in order to walk through it freely, at my own pace, and after having prepared myself by copious reading.

On this twofold point, I kept my promise. In the course of the following weeks, I devoured the few books on art, and on aesthetics in general, that I could find in the little library for *khâgneux*. *The Voices of Silence* towered above the rest, being thought at that time, by those whom I considered (and who considered themselves) "connoisseurs," as the last word on the subject. I plunged into it, giving Malraux a central place in my plan of accelerated education. I thought I'd become very learned because I now knew how to distinguish the main phases in the history of Western painting, because I could, if the occasion arose, hold forth on a few themes in the philosophy of art. I even took care to write down and memorize the expressions that seemed to me correct or brilliant. One of them, at least, has remained in my memory, one I'd found somewhere, and which was later to do me service for a long time – practically up to the present: "A work of art is a representation, not of a world, but of a worldview." Equipped with this baggage, I returned to the museum for two or three additional visits. Still brief and superficial ones. Then I didn't have time to continue.

But with Tamara, I was sure, things would be different. Thanks to her, I would be able to find the key to everything that had previously eluded me. However, the first expedition we made together was hardly encouraging. Was it the presence of my friend, so close to me, vibrant in a mauve dress I'd never seen on her before, that troubled me? Was it the memory, which immediately surged up, of our tête-à-têtes the preceding year that prevented me from concentrating on what we were looking at? Probably a bit of both. In any case, I quickly had to admit that the artistic veneer I thought I'd given myself was inoperative. In front of a painting, I was lost. My few references, bookish or abstract, got mixed up. Impossible to name what I was seeing, since, as before, I continued not to see anything. Which was pretty clearly shown by my sheepish silence when confronted by the remarks – often enthusiastic, sometimes skeptical, very rarely negative – that the contemplation of each new canvas elicited from my friend. She soon noticed this, and was at first astonished by it. I didn't know what to say. But she immediately found an explanation: it was normal, she thought, that my eye, accustomed to the contrasts in color and the sharp dissonances that for her characterized Africa, would at first have some difficulty in getting its bearings in the grayness of the museum; all that could only be a matter of time, of getting used to it. And, patiently, gently, she undertook to retrain my eyes. She was triumphant – in a modest way, of course, and through a simple accentuation of her smile – when after a few Sundays she saw that I was making progress. Like her, I was able to stop before a canvas by an unknown painter, study it at length with an attentive eye, examine this or that detail, and then, after a moment of reflection, mention the series of references that made it possible to situate it, the whole into which it could be integrated. I was happy to show my aptitude for perceiving as she did, at first glance or almost, what she called the geometrical organization of a picture, for grasping the peculiarities in the detail of the design, in the treatment of light and color, and for locating the differences and resemblances between two neighboring works. And thus it was that we became real regulars.

I cannot, even today, forget the blithe happiness of these escapades. I tried to give an account of them, as they occurred, with all the rigor and precision that seemed to me at that time indispensable.

Spring 1959

Here you are again, the two of you, in the Louvre, that is, more or less at home. You're striding confidently down the Grande Galérie, at the end of which Titian's Francis I, like several dozen visitors shifting their weight from one foot to another, seems absorbed in the contemplation of the Mona Lisa: no doubt he's wondering about those blocks of stone in the background of the picture, about those mountains that seem to have come from another planet, or about those rushing streams as sinuous as the lips that bear the excessively famous smile. You pay no attention to all that, and you launch into your own explorations.

You have a weakness for Greek antiquities, to which you ritually devote the initial phase of your visit. Tamara feels connected to this world, toward which she's borne by a kind of instinct. She confided to you that as a child she dreamed of walking, with her father and her uncle, along the banks of the Ilissos, dipping her bare feet in the current, or else climbing, perched on the shoulders of one of them, the slopes of Olympus and the Pindus range in the coolness of an April morning. But above all she is now attracted by the Athens of Phidias and Pericles.

Every time you go together into these rooms, you recall the words she whispered in your ear one day: "J'aime le souvenir de ces époques nues" (her Baudelaire is not exactly Violetta's!), to which you replied, of course, "Dont Phébus se plaisait à dorer les statues."[44] It's true that you loved those statues! On their faces, you followed, from room to room, a whole history: the grim and formal faces of the archaic period, the birth and gradual blooming of the smile — that luminous smile, the sign of a relationship to the world characterized by love (you can't help comparing it briefly to that of your friend) — that will soon yield to expressions marked by doubt, concern, and then outright melancholy. Tamara is often sorry that she can't admire these sculptures in the state in which their contemporaries saw them: living and close to them, like the familiar objects they then were. The almost complete disappearance of the colors touches her like a personal loss. She sometimes tries to find on the marble the traces of the skilful conjunction of red or blue, ochre or vermilion. Naturally, you think you have to feel as she does on this point, although to tell the truth it matters less to you than it does to her. But you are able, at other moments, to have a less consensual attitude.

Thus you were proud, a few days ago, to show her (at first, a little to provoke her, but then with growing conviction as you spoke) how much certain objects of this period had benefited from being detached from their context: when, miraculously preserved, some fragment of a statue (this head, this torso, this calf, this foot), far from appearing to be a simple bit of debris, seems to have concentrated in itself all the perfection of the original sculpture; or, on the contrary, when the broken, mutilated remains of a bas-relief (this vague silhouette, is it that of a priestess, a bacchante, or a flute-player?) seems to have been able to draw, from the very violence they've suffered, an additional seductiveness. As if, you added on a sudden inspiration, erosion or destruction had been the artist's accomplices, entrusted with giving birth to a more powerful, more concentrated work, more in accord, in short, with what you sense is becoming, from week to week, your special taste: a bit of pathos to spice up the excessively serene purity of the classics. And this time it was she who applauded.

When you'd passed through the rooms devoted to antiquities, you sometimes took long strolls through the painting galleries, without fatigue, before discovering your prey. Little by little, you'd learned to find your way through the underbrush of canvases piled up any old way, often poorly illuminated, and presented in an order whose logic escapes you. Suddenly, your eyes light up and you stop in front of paintings you've never seen, and which seem to be waiting for your visit. They have that je ne sais quoi of gravity and discretion that coincides exactly with your idea of the beautiful. Yesterday, it was those two portraits of Mallarmé, one by Renoir, the other by Monet: perfect, both of them, and yet so different! You concluded that they said a great deal more about their painters than about their model. "As if each of the painters had tried to focus on only those traits in the poet that he could use to translate his own personality," you immediately explained.

You have in common — this is one of those coincidences whose discovery enchants you — a taste for the vast compositions that spread over a whole wall, in a mysterious throng, their mythological heroes, their fantastic bestiaries, their allegorical figures. You like to decipher them, and in order to do *so, you take pleasure in combining your efforts, in blending your competencies. Some of them immediately give up their secret, while others, which are in that respect more exciting, seem at first to reject your penetration. But it suffices that one of you succeeds in mastering a single element (Mercury's caduceus, a bacchante's thyrsis, Venus's dove) in order for all the others, successively losing their mystery, to open up without difficulty. You engage in this exercise with seriousness, the same that you applied, last year, to translating the words of certain cantatas* (Schlage doch, gewünschte Stunde), *certain Lieder* (Taubenpost) *or the libretto of the Magic Flute. It's a kind of seriousness that surprises and irritates other visitors; those who probably justify their lack of curiosity by proclaiming that in these matters it is not necessary to understand everything, that it's quite enough to feel. Occasionally, a detail strikes you. Sometimes by its exactitude: the grace of a baby's gesture, the expression of amazement on a goddess's face, the harmonious fall of a figure's hair. Sometimes by its misplaced, incongruous character. For instance, last Sunday, there was a session in front of a large Mantegna entitled* Parnassus or the Dance of the Muses, *which ended in uncontrollable laughter: wearied, no doubt, by the effort you'd just made, you couldn't help finding ridiculous an unfortunate Pegasus, as hairy as a bear, covered from his hooves to his chest with black spots like a giraffe, tangled up in wings too big for him ("it looks just like the Albatross,[45]" she said, giggling), and who seemed to be giving his neighbor, Mercury, a look full of reproach . . .*

These visits, which were taking a more and more erudite turn, further increased our complicity, transforming it into intellectual intimacy. In this way we succeeded in elaborating, regarding art, a sort of catechism for our private use, whose points long remained for me articles of faith. But all these shared thoughts did not cause us to make any progress in love. As if a wall continued to separate that world from the other.

However, it was hard for us, in certain rooms, to avoid a confrontation with the flesh, in its most seductive, and sometimes in its most aggressive, form: goddesses, one after another, in their sculptural nudity, heroines painted in the simple garb of their beauty. I recall standing often and long in front of *Antiope's Slumber* or *Le Concert Champêtre*, our favorites. We tried to keep our composure, to show that we were not embarrassed by these floods of amorous bodies, by the daring of an age that was able to combine beauty and sensual pleasure. I'd even invented a little game for us – "the catalogue game": the point was, after having chosen the painting together, to describe it in the most complete and concise manner possible. A sentence or two, no more, like a listing in a catalogue. Achieving this required multiple revisions and mutual corrections. Sometimes, however, we came across canvases in front of which we limited ourselves to exchanging obviously ironic looks, which were supposed to cleanse us of any suspicion of prudishness. But we abstained from any commentary. As if the fear of having to say certain words tied our tongues in knots. A brief episode, duly transcribed the same evening, will give an idea of how great, in this kind of situation, our embarrassment still was.

Spring 59

The Louvre, again. Today a rather bizarre composition attracted your attention. At first sight, it was a group of women, more or less flat-chested, fighting with . . . little children; some are even brandishing lances against them! Of course, you were both very puzzled by such a cruel representation. You were even on the point of reacting, not yet knowing whether you should be scandalized by it or ridicule it. But before making your gibes, you took the precaution of looking at the picture's title. And that was enough to shut your mouths. The canvas is by Perugino. It's called The Combat of Love and Chastity.

On coming out of the museum, I dreamed more and more often of a less sophisticated, more candid eroticism, of the kind that is shown without prudishness in Indian sculptures – Krishna's frolics, in the middle of a forest, with very appetizing female cowherds – reproductions of which I'd seen in a bookstore in the Rue Bonaparte. Why, I lamented, have we been unable to take anything from a culture that was concerned to that extent with the glorification of pleasure, of the opportunities offered to desire?

16

Galahad

This situation, despite the dreams and languor it brought with it, could not last. I absolutely had to get out of it, by some strategy other than waiting. Since, I told myself, I am once again impeded – as I was at the same point in the preceding year – by my uncertainty regarding Tamara's feelings, I have to give her an opportunity to show them clearly. Call her bluff. Force her to confess the love that I myself am clearly unable to express. For that purpose, it seemed to me, I had to take advantage of the opportunities that the circumstances once again offered, as they had at the same point in the preceding year. The idea occurred to me that I could make use of some of the afternoons that, temporarily giving up the museum, we devoted to so-called work sessions. These were more or less scholarly conversations on subjects connected with her studies. They always focused on art, or rather on the arts, their contribution to knowledge, their relationship to pleasure. Moments during which I had time to exhibit the rhetorical virtuosity that *khâgne* was supposed to provide. Tamara consulted me, received my opinions favorably, imbued herself with my views. With a confidence that filled me with pride and gave me the feeling of existing more intensely. I still remember a disquisition on "the useful and the pleasurable." I suggested a compromise formula, like the ones that I shamelessly used in my school essays. "There is not necessarily any contradiction, you see. Literature, for example: it is because it is pleasurable that it can sometimes be useful." And I did not fail to trot out my favorite model, Scheherazade, who was able to save her life – and those of all the queens for one night who would have followed her – solely through the pleasure that her stories gave the sultan Shariar. Another time, it was the baroque's turn: she quickly came to agree with me that it should be presented not as a specific school, but rather as a historical constant, present in times and places that were sometimes far removed from each other, from the Venetian glaziers to Guimard's metro stations. Sometimes, our conversations on these subjects took the form of real jousting. A pretext for a friendly battle on reversed fronts: I gave myself the pleasure of taking her by surprise by advancing the rigid opinions I thought most likely to satisfy her, she replied by adopting the flexible positions she knew were more in accord with my views.

At such moments, I felt I was reliving my first afternoons with Violetta, when concern for our dignity led us into discussions that helped us postpone the time of our amorous frolics. The difference was that with Tamara, the culmination of our debates was a common activity of another kind, reading.

May 59

These notes, put down in haste, in order to preserve some trace of your reading sessions. Reading, for you and in this new springtime, refers exclusively to poetry. You admire the range (and the diversity!) of Tamara's knowledge in this domain. Like Sonia, and like Fabrice as well, she can mention competently names as foreign to the academic world, and as little familiar to your own ear, as those of Milosz, Supervielle, Reverdy, Cendrars, Max Jacob . . . It's enough to make you think her aptitude for feeling and her faculty of marveling have no limits! Far more than you, she is sensitive to everything that escapes the calculated adjustments of language. You're astonished, you're even frightened sometimes, by her enthusiasm for the ineffable, the indefinite, the impalpable. She'd love to make you forget your excessively rigid ideas, to make you admit that poetry is not only a matter of language, but consubstantial with things, only their hidden side. She has collected a few of the maxims of which she is, like you, fond (no doubt because they sometimes allow you to avoid direct avowals!). Last Sunday: "The poetic word is a murmur." This week: "Poetry is humanity's original religion." You wonder whether her emphasis on this latter assertion — which she may have, just think of it, thought up for your benefit — isn't a way of making you understand that your poetic entente does away, in her eyes, with all the differences between you.

Moments of grace. Shut away in her bedroom, your backs to the window, facing the fireplace, you begin by pushing your armchairs closer to each other.

She takes from the table next to the bed a large bound volume, always the same one. It's an anthology, of which she knows large portions by heart. She quickly flips through the pages to find the text she wants to show you today. And she immediately gives it to you to read. Her hand, holding the book open before your eyes, is very close. You can feel her shoulder against yours, and sometimes even, against your chest, the movements of her outstretched arm, which occasionally take the form of an almost imperceptible trembling. The real ceremony can then begin. A ceremony that is usually silent. No need for you to raise your voice, sometimes no need even to speak at all. She keeps her eyes on you the whole time you're reading, taking pleasure in deciphering on your lips the very words she is reciting to herself. When it happens that you also know by heart the text she has chosen, she gives a little cry of joy, for that's another proof of what you one day called your pre-established harmony. Then she puts down the book. Each of you, your eyes riveted on the other's mouth, pronounces, softly, one by one, the words of the poem. And then in an instant the verses murmured in common transport you, as had the dance on the evening of the party, into another world.

That form of intimacy was precisely the one of which I now wanted to take advantage. Why should it be doomed to remain exclusive of any other? Why shouldn't it play, on the contrary, the role of a foundation or starting point? I searched in literature for situations comparable to our own that might serve us as a model for finally giving our story the natural consequences so long in coming. I then recalled one scene, no doubt the most famous of all scenes of reading together: that in which Paolo Malatesta and Francesca da Rimini, reading together in all innocence the romance of Lancelot and Queen Guinevere, suddenly become aware of their love. Which Francesca's shade, in her poignant tale, sums up in a simple verse, one of the rare verses of Dante's *Inferno* that I knew at the time:

"Galeotto fu il libro e chi lo scrisse"[46]

But for us, I wondered, what accomplice poem, what compassionate author would play Galahad's role? Where would I find the text that could serve to reveal our love to us, to mediate for us, to lead us, like Paolo and Francesca, to a kiss, and beyond? I dreamed of making come the day of which we could later say, as they had: "On that day, we did not feel the need to read further." Even if it was from some circle of Hell . . .

It was not necessary for me to take that route. Chance, or perhaps Providence, once again, came to my aid.

17

The Way Out

It was, despite the fact that spring had come, a cool and misty Sunday afternoon. Tamara, as sometimes happened, was alone in the apartment. A fire she had made herself just before Manuel's arrival lit up the room. On the program for the day was not the Louvre, but rather the Bibliothèque Nationale, for an exhibit of Daumier's drawings. Sonia, who had gone to the opening the preceding Tuesday, had urged them to go discover an artist whom, repeating with enthusiasm an expression of Michelet's that appeared in the catalogue, she called "the Michelangelo of caricature." But the dismal weather dissuaded them.

They were on the point of sitting down, after having moved close to the fireplace the two armchairs that were now side by side, facing the flames. Manuel was beginning to feel the warmth of the fire on his face, and on his ears as well, which he felt getting hot and turning purple at the same time. "Good Lord, what an image of me Tamara is going to have," he said to himself uneasily. To make sure he didn't look too ridiculous, he glanced furtively toward the mirror over the mantelpiece. But what he saw in it, as if for first time, was Tamara's bed, with its light-colored spread embroidered with large white flowers and, side-by-side on the bolster, two twin pillows that seemed to be smiling at him in their batiste slips.

Then something broke loose inside him. Something sudden. A flood of words. Violent. Irresistible. It sometimes – rarely, in moments of extreme tension – happened that he had to let his voice run ahead of him, and he followed far behind, as if it were outside him. It was with that voice, which had become metallic and neutral, that he began, without daring to take his eyes off the mirror, a short speech, as brutal as it was improvised. All his accumulated recriminations went whirling into it. He spoke about the coldness, the reserve, or rather, no, the polite indifference Tamara had shown him since the beginning of the year. About the disappointment, and then the bitterness, he'd felt. About the fact that he was going to be forced to put an early end to their meetings, which had obviously become a burden on her, though she did not yet have courage to say so . . .

"A burden . . . A burden . . ."

Without responding to what she had just heard, Tamara, pale with surprise, repeated these words several times. In a low voice. Slowly shaking her head, in a way that seemed to express lassitude and sadness as much as denial. Then suddenly she turned toward the fire, putting both rounded palms over her eyes, as if to protect them from the heat. And he thought he clearly saw, shining on her pink cheeks, the trace of two tears.

He looked at her, at first incredulous, then overwhelmed.

He should probably have thrown himself at her feet, asked her pardon, explained to her that of course – she knew it better than anyone – he didn't believe a word of these absurd reproaches, which were only the clumsy echo of his concern, his impatience. Or else, on the contrary – and this is what all those romantic heroes he despaired of being able to imitate would certainly have done – he should have, in a sacred silence, the only thing befitting the gravity of the moment, taken her in his arms and covered her face, still slightly damp and salty, with all the kisses that had so long awaited their hour. She, after a brief instant of surprise, would surely, and with very good grace, have allowed him to do so. Then, emboldened by her friend's daring, she would have freely given him kiss for kiss, caress for caress. Thus they would have remained for a long time, repeating indefatigably all the gestures of love and tenderness they had never yet even hinted at. And, many years later, they would both have continued to cherish the memory of these tears, of this silence, of these kisses, as much as the greatest moments in their singular love story.

But there are people whom the strength of their feelings emboldens, and others whom this same force paralyzes. At the time, all he could do was remain motionless, mute. Conscious only of having become the spectator of a process that he had been careless enough to set in motion without gauging its risks, without foreseeing its outcome. And the only thought that passed, for an instant, through the void of his mind was this one: finally he understood why, in the stories his mother had told him, and that had illuminated his childhood, the tears that fell from the eyes of a beloved woman were transformed into diamonds.

Tamara hastened to swallow her tears, resumed almost without effort her smiling face. As if he hadn't said anything, as if nothing had happened, she started asking him questions about his work that week, though she emphasized – with a slight touch of irony – the state of nervous tension in which the approach of the competitive examinations seemed to have put him. He quickly understood that he had to let her believe that he had seen nothing, but he had far more difficulty than she in recovering his spirits. To his suppressed confusion was soon added, almost in spite of himself, a strange rush of pride. Weren't those tears the finest of trophies? It was he who had provoked them, he alone. They were his work, incontestably. The result of the words he had spoken. And they had the merit of providing him, in the most eloquent of ways, the message he'd been so long waiting for. No, his beloved was not solely a statue of ivory and coral: everything did not slip off the carapace of placid good will, indulgent serenity, and inflexible sweetness that occasionally exasperated him. No, the visits he made to her were not in any way burdens on her. There was no reason not to think they were precious to her, on the contrary. That she awaited them, and secretly prepared herself for them. Who knew, perhaps even on that very day, intoxicated by the powerful flow of the shower on her skin, after having soaped, one after another, her two breasts, then her stomach and her thighs, she had gone, still wet (a few drops of water stubbornly clinging to the hollow of her loins), to contemplate naked before the mirror the perfection of her body, and to instill in a few secret places known only to herself, a tiny bit of her favorite perfume. Perhaps she had, for just an instant, let her hand wander from her breasts to her hips, from her hips to her pubis, in a slow and dreamy caress. Perhaps she had then meditated on each detail of her toilette, checking her hair, the narrow pleats of her plaid skirt, the buckle on her belt, the depth of her décolletage, worried about the impression she was going to make on her friend, that friend who was being so slow to take the masculine initiatives she was waiting for. Perhaps . . . In any case, Manuel was now sure that she was attached to him by something strong and that she rejected with as much feeling as he did the idea of breaking off their relationship.

This certainty filled him, all during the following week, with a tranquil courage. Now, the circumstances were favorable. Now, he no longer risked being rebuffed. And even if there was still a risk, Manuel felt ready to assume it. Was he committing a crime by desiring her? By showing her that he did? By telling her so in the clearest way? All the poems and all the songs in the world have been saying nothing else since time began . . . If she refused to listen to him after the scene the other day, then, too bad! He'd have to give up hope of ever seeing her come back to a healthy, normal, human attitude. Then, as Fabrice had put it one day, "Mademoiselle was preparing herself for a career as a saint. In the area of ecstasies and swoons. In the *upper room*, in short." In that case, and in that case alone, he would give up the fight. How could he follow her to such heights? But he soon set aside these apprehensions. They were no longer appropriate. Those two precious tears, which had appeared abruptly and were as abruptly wiped away, were signs of the most explicit kind, still more encouraging than had been, the preceding spring, the whole evening of the party.

It remained to find the form in which he would make his declaration. He had thought only too much, for months, about the problem. But the circumstances were no longer the same as they had been the preceding year. What should he do now not to remain far below, far short of what the situation required? He had to find words that could be more than words. Limpid, radiant words. Words full of vigor, of energy. But what word would ever have the power of a tear? Even the words of the *Song of Songs* seemed to him inadequate to the task.

And then all of a sudden, right in the middle of the library, when he's leafing through a book on surrealism, he comes across the sentence an earlier reader had underlined and circled in red: "We will reduce art to its simplest expression, which is love." Manuel is not sure he understands it. But it strikes him. Its three main words spring out of their context and begin spinning around with increasing speed in his head: art, expression, love, art, expression, love . . . Then, in an instant, the solution emerges in its luminous simplicity. And with it, a plan of action, which he writes down as if it were a genuine assignment. Sure this time of success, he does not hesitate to give this page the name *The Way Out*.

May 59

How could you have failed to think of it earlier, fool that you are? Since she likes art so much, since it is in the museum alone that she's willing to look the body and sex in the face, you've finally realized that it's from that fact that you have to start. The Louvre! What finer setting for a declaration, what finer love nest than this palace, which you have, thanks to her, made your own? And what better instrument, for showing your desire, than universal painting, in its most suggestive productions? This is the time to test (in vivo, so to speak) the principle that Tamara herself has acknowledged: one of the functions of art is to embody our phantasms, to display in broad daylight what each of us conceals.

So you're going, for once, to take things in hand. Leave nothing to chance. And transform your next visit into a regular tour of love.

You will review one by one, with Tamara, the stages that lead from the first glance to the first kiss, and from the first kiss to the first embrace: a set of paintings that, if they were brought together in a single room, would constitute the most voluptuous of private collections.

You will take care to include, in each of these stages, only universally celebrated paintings, as famous for the mastery they display as for the sensuality or eroticism that emerges from them (you'll leave aside, please, at least this time, the hair-splitting debates about the distinction between the sensual and the erotic, and other nonsense of the same ilk).

You will try — a refinement Tamara cannot fail to appreciate — to have, all through your tour, as many heroines as possible whose faces may in some respect be thought to resemble her own. That should not be too difficult for you now. Some time ago, you acquired the habit of projecting, instinctively, her features onto the women's faces you see, without distinguishing centuries or schools. So you'll be prepared to discern — and to make her perceive — for your enthusiasm cannot fail to be contagious — a little of her presence in some of your oldest acquaintances: Isabella d'Este, Simonetta Vespucci, Joan of Aragon. Or else, with a syncretism you find enchanting, in Bathsheba as much as in Diana. Not to mention, finally, one or another of Fragonard's Bathers or Titian's Young Woman at Her Toilet.

You will stop in front of each of the chosen paintings, and, adopting the most natural voice you can (but if a little ill-suppressed emotion alters your delivery, don't worry about it too much), you will first exclaim over the perfection of an anatomy, the beauty of the movement of an arm folded to conceal a breast, or perhaps (you'll know how to suggest this) to accentuate it.

Next, you will not hesitate to show how the Dianas and the Danaës, the Venuses, Ledas, and Bathshebas flaunt, without any shame, their smooth and supple bellies, their mature bosoms, their proud flanks, their luscious limbs.

You will emphasize the assurance that seems to be given all these creatures, at the moment they are about to give themselves over to love, by the possession of a body that, thanks to the painter's complicity, one can divine, even in its most intimate recesses, as perfect.

As you go along, you will point out the eyes — by turns supplicating and voluptuous — of some of these heroines, who, while abandoning themselves to the most carnal love, seem to be contemplating something they see elsewhere, beyond our world.

Then you will come to all those women about whom you will say that they know how to bring to its extreme culmination what you will not be afraid to call, at the end of your tour, the fusion of erotic ecstasy with mystical ecstasy.

You will utter each of your words, each of your sentences, and especially the last ones, with complete conviction: you will be convincing only if you are sincere.

Sincere, he promised himself he would be sincere. And without much effort. What man in love was ever more sincere than he was at this moment?

Several nights in a row, he dreamed lovingly of this project, which he considered as respectful as it was audacious. "Exactly what's needed for her," he repeated to himself with satisfaction. In order to put it into effect, he'd chosen a symbolic moment: the first anniversary of "the party," the party that remained for him the luminous point to which they had to return.

18

Repetition

I'm sure you've recognized, reader, another product of my old effort to write a novel, although I cannot give the precise date when it was composed. But I'm not sure that, all through this passage, you've shared my hero's contradictory emotions. His confusion, then his pride (a little suspect, all the same, don't you think?) regarding the tears he involuntarily caused his friend to shed. His enthusiasm for the strange plan he finally elaborated. However, there's nothing more in accord, I solemnly swear, with the true facts. For a long time it has been known and repeated that the true can sometimes be implausible. So I can go on with my story, without having to change one iota in the preceding chapter.

What came, then, of this marvelous plan? Well, quite simply, nothing. I did not have a chance to make the liberating tour, the triumphal itinerary I'd described with so much energy. No, the masterpieces of the Louvre were not able to seize the opportunity I offered them finally to show the younger generations, in an irrefutable manner, their practical utility: art did not have the privilege of serving the expression of love. For my outings with Tamara were suddenly interrupted. As she had the preceding year, at about the same time, my friend ceased to communicate with me. No more letters, no *pneumatiques*, nothing. I'd lost her, I'd found her again, and now she'd escaped me once more.

It was written, then, that I would have to relive the agonies of anxiety, the torments of waiting. This time, however, my reaction was more sensible. Certainly, I could have told myself that nothing dries more easily than a girl's tears, and lost myself again in conjectures on my friend's shameful fickleness. But I didn't. I didn't give way to a fit of either rage or jealousy. I didn't blame any rival, suspected no ill will, no family obstacle. Without hesitation, I made the diagnosis that seemed to me obvious: illness. The preceding year's experience had done at least that much for me. But that experience in no way alleviated my suffering. Quite the contrary.

First, I had to endure Fabrice's incredulity and sarcasm. All he could do was scoff.

"Ha, ha! So she's dared to pull the disappearing trick on you again? She's got nerve, your little saint! But don't worry too much. I'll bet things are going to be all right, and before long, just like the last time, she'll be back. In five or six weeks she'll be telling you that she was gripped by some kind of spasms. And you'll be ready for another round ... That said, you should take advantage of this to get yourself out of this whole thing. Believe me, as people say, you have to know how to end a strike ..."

My confusion grew still greater when a note from Sonia, to whom I'd finally gone to ask for news, came to tell me, at the beginning of June, that Tamara had had an unexpected relapse, that it was preferable that I not write to her at the moment, and that she would probably not be back in Paris before the end of the summer. Thus I lost her at the very moment when I no longer doubted her love and before I'd been able to tell her how strong mine was.

The repercussions of this disaster on my academic life were immediate. The season for the competitive entrance examination for the Rue d'Ulm – the real examination, this time – had arrived. Tortured by concern over my friend, a concern that quite quickly turned into fear, I was not, to say the least, in the most appropriate state of mind. I failed several tests, in particular the one on philosophy. It is true that the subject set, "Repetition," hardly favored me. From any point of view. At first, it surprised me by its extreme density, in my view excessive: where should one start to discuss this multifaceted word? It didn't really lend itself to the little verbal games – etymological or others – by means of which I usually got by, and which risked drawing a blank in this case. Above all, it wounded me as a sordid irony of fate directed at me. I couldn't help applying the word to my own situation. It is a fact that I was currently experiencing, against my will, the pure and simple repetition of my disappointment the preceding year. But while I was analyzing it, this situation itself suddenly appeared to me, in a disquieting premonition, as being a model, a genuine matrix, for the whole rest of my love life. And I saw myself already doomed to repeat endlessly my initial failure!

For a moment, I was tempted to draw on this still stinging experience to carry out a reflection on my own relationship to time. To investigate in depth the meaning of this abrupt "return of the same" that, in this domain as in others, seemed to be pursuing me. But I didn't dare launch into it. Only Fabrice was capable of that sort of boldness; he knew how to connect, through a series of brilliant formulas, the humblest incident of his personal life with the loftiest metaphysical speculations. So I wrote without enthusiasm a few superficial pages, on which floated, bound together by a slender theoretical tegument, memories of my most recent readings: Nietzsche, Kierkegaard, and Proust. Then, far before the end of the six hours the examination rules allowed us, I was the first to leave the room, under the surprised and disapproving gaze of all my friends, in order to go wait, sitting in front of a hot chocolate in the bistro in the Rue des Feuillantines, for the end of the test. At the beginning of July, I learned, without surprise, that I had failed. Many of my fellow students, who'd not had the same problems I'd had (but then, what did I know? They were just as discreet about their love affairs as I was) were in the same situation. Which attenuated only slightly my disappointment.

A year lost. So I had to prepare myself to redo a *khâgne*. Persevere in the condition of a schoolboy. In this domain as well, nothing had been achieved, everything had to be begun over again. Clearly, my life in Paris was increasingly taking the form of a dreary marching in place.

As a consolation, I allotted myself, at the urging of Ariane, to whom I'd sent a letter she found alarming (so alarming, in fact, that she did not dare show it to my parents!), a week of real rest. "Take advantage of being in Paris, then, you big lout," she ordered me. "It's now or never."

I decided to devote these days of vacation, the first I'd had in months, to a movie cure. I was led to do this by two old friends,

Simon and Henri, whom I had run into by chance one hot evening on the terrace of the Capoulade. They, at least, were not worrying about their studies! Right at the beginning of the school year, they'd deliberately traded the constraints of khâgne for the great freedom of the students at the Sorbonne.[47] In June, Simon had not even bothered to take the one examination in general sociology for which he had registered: he'd simply overslept. The only thing that interested them was systematically scouring the movie houses of Paris, from Barbès to Passy, from Gobelins to the Bastille, in search of the unknown masterpiece. One after the other, we saw together La Nuit des forains, Le Plaisir (twice), Ordet, The Seven Samurai (one and one-half times), The Cabinet of Dr. Caligari, and, to crown everything, Hiroshima mon amour (twice). They were far more enthusiastic about this last film than I was. Right away, they discerned in it an epic meditation, the itinerary of a consciousness (and many other subtleties that had, I admit, escaped me), to the point that they decided to devote a major study to it: they were sure they could show that it was a pre-revolutionary film. For my part, I was a thousand miles away from any such concerns.

In a hurry to get away, I even gave up the pleasures of another sea crossing, and without telling anyone, took a night flight for Casablanca.

July 59

Not a very glorious return, you can certainly say that much! The child prodigy brings back in his luggage only a big academic failure (the first one) and (what else can one call it?) an enormous unhappiness in love. Shipwreck all along the line . . .

Ariane, who with her usual intuition seems to have understood, even though you don't tell her everything, consoles you as well as she can. Once again, she works hard to get you out of your melancholy. Without much success, for you cooperate with her hardly at all. As for your friends here, astonished to see you still bogged down in what they've always catalogued as an incomprehensible and hopeless adventure, they have started harassing you again. Their remarks wound you. But you don't have the strength to reply. You're no longer sure they're wrong. Who knows? What you've taken *up to now for incomprehension, or even ill will, may only be, after all, clear-sightedness.*

After Sonia's disquieting and not very explicit letter, I'd had no further news of Tamara. Just in case, I'd sent a note to inform her that I'd failed the examinations, and returned to Morocco. Then, after a period of great, daily anguish, which lasted several weeks, I'd finally resigned myself to waiting indefinitely. My teeth clenched, my heart closed. It would do no good to write. I sensed that, as in the preceding year, my letters would not be given to her, or else she would not be allowed to reply to them. Which didn't prevent me from thinking about her, in violent spurts. So violent that sometimes I could no longer contain myself. I had to fill the void within me, at any cost. I found, at those moments, only one remedy to bring my lovely absent one back to me: I pronounced one by one, in a low voice, repeating them ceaselessly, as I had seen done during my childhood, the letters, or rather the syllables, of her first name, and their sonorities, as if by magic, calmed me. They even restored to me, eventually, something of her image.

Then I tried to transport myself in thought into the room, her bedroom, where we had so often sat together, to reconstruct with precision the setting. The bed. The big white flowers on the embroidered bedspread. The two armchairs covered in light-colored rep. The mahogany pedestal table, slightly rickety (you had to put a shim under it to make it stand straight), covered with bound books. The gilded mirror over the mantelpiece. In their dark wood frames, the three romantic engravings, one of which, the middle one, represents a young woman getting out of her bath. The music box in which she kept the few pieces of jewelry (solely in silver, that was what went best with the paleness of her complexion) that she sometimes wore on our outings. Sweltering under the sun on my stretch of deserted beach, I was constantly visiting this place, which my imagination had already transformed into a kind of sanctuary, seeing again our last afternoon, and reliving the unforeseeable and precious scene of the tears, on which, despite the fact that it had not embodied any of my expectations, I continued to feed.

141

That was when my need to bring Tamara near me began to take another form. A very strange form.

10 August 59

Tamara, these words that you will never read, these words are addressed only to you. Today I made an important resolution, which concerns both of us. You see, it's no longer enough for me to imagine here, through my memories, each of the features of your face, each of the pieces of furniture in your bedroom, each of the trifling objects with which you've surrounded yourself (as if for me anything that has to do with you could be trifling!). I want to go far beyond, far deeper. One of the last images I have of you is of your tears. Yes, you don't know that I know, but that's how it is, I know. You wept because of me, the finest present you've ever given me, before sending me off to solitude and sadness. Impossible to ignore that instant. I want, on the contrary, to rediscover what led you to shed those tears. Who knows how long ago they'd been formed in you, how long you held them in! So I'm going to try to go back, step by step, to their source. And in order to do so, to reconstitute, day by day, how you might have changed since our first meeting. In other words, I want to substitute myself for you, my sweet love. Get into your mind. Slip into your heart. To follow there, commingled with you, the steps of your internal struggles. Yes, to find out (finally!) how you see our story. A crazy task, of course. Commensurate with my madness. You can count on me to carry it out.

With what energy, and what application, I set about my strange work! I devoted to it the hottest hours of the day, which I thereby took away from despondency. From the outset, the text I began to produce took the form of a diary. My main concern was to give it all the marks of verisimilitude. So I had obliged myself to fill it, as much as possible, with sentences my friend had actually written or uttered, extracts from works she had actually read. I had some resources. I had only to take up the notes I'd more and more frequently scribbled to keep some record of our meetings, to look through the books I knew had marked her. It seemed to me that in coinciding very nearly with her in the act of writing, by weaving our contributions closely together, I would attain the only form of possession that remained open to me. This exercise provided me with moments of genuine pleasure. I considered a page completed only when, on rereading the fragments that constituted it, I could no longer distinguish what was hers from what was mine.

Completely absorbed in my fever to write and in the problems it posed for me, I paid scarcely any attention to the use I might make of these pages.

Just in case, I carefully copied them out in a pretty notebook with a thick green cover, of the Mektoub brand, which Ariane had brought back from Rabat for me. It was only much later that an idea I liked occurred to me: constructing a book that could serve them as a setting, a novel in which this set of fragments that I henceforth called The Green Notebook would be included. An idea that was never to leave me again, inciting me to pursue the exercise from one year to the next.

The summer ended in this way. Less melancholically than it had begun.

October soon came. I had to go back. Resume, without enthusiasm, the routine of the Lycée, but resolved to do everything to be sure that this year would be the last.

The fall passed quickly.

A heavy program. Greek, Latin, English. Translations, preparations. Literary essays. Philosophical essays. Historical essays. Oral examinations. Constant reading. The sole distraction: going to the movies, on rare occasions, with Fabrice or Violetta. I had not a minute to bemoan my fate, as I had so often done the other years.

I was absolutely certain that some day or other Tamara would get in touch with me. She couldn't not do it. I just had to wait.

19
Third Year

It was only at the beginning of December that a completely new messenger – for the wobbling, lurching Eugène (called Hugène, called Gégène, called The Gross) had finally been asked to go drink somewhere else – that a new messenger, then still without a nickname, brought me, without any ceremony, the *pneumatique* I'd never stopped waiting for. So Tamara had remained faithful to our old mode of communication! That seemed to me a good sign, even if the content of the message was rather limited. My friend told me that she had returned to Paris; she wanted to tell me that my setback in July should not discourage me, that it was rare that one was accepted the first time around, and that I was right to make another attempt; and finally, that we could see each other soon.

So we got together again. After more than six months of complete silence. Still another new phase in our relationship was about to begin. A phase even more singular than the earlier ones, and one whose main lines I have been able, by juxtaposing various fragments from the period, to reconstitute.

Saturday, 12. The joy of getting back together. A joy clearly shared. Tamara's smile when she greets you! Her eagerness to make you sit down in "your" chair. You have the impression, this time, that what is essential between you has not grown old, has not changed. This long forced slumber, far from having eroded your affection, seems to have helped it remain intact. Ready to go back into action at any time. And you are inclined not to mess up this new departure.

Second visit. Once the euphoria of getting together again, of exchanging affectionate phrases, has passed, you were moved by the pallor of her face, the new lassitude that her voice occasionally betrays. While she was talking, you glanced rapidly at the mirror. As if you expected to find there a trace, a residue, of her tears last spring.

You're going to have to have to come down to earth. No, your conviction that a rebirth of your friendship was possible, imminent, did not last, unfortunately. The circumstances hardly favored it. No question of outings, at this point. Neither as a twosome nor as a threesome. Tamara is trying to catch up on all the university work she missed. This requires that she make great efforts, which have to be followed by periods of almost complete rest. You don't have much free time yourself.

Is this really the time to speak of love to her? Of this love whose magnitude you can measure by the current acuteness of your suffering. You wanted, from the first day forward, to have a decisive discussion with her on this subject. Once again, you prefer to postpone it. Moreover, what good would it do, now? You have placed her love far too high, as if on a throne of porphyry and gold, to have any serious hope that she will descend as far as you. So you talk about other things. She does too.

For the last few days, there has been an intruder in your conversations: the Desert (yes, with a capital "D"). She keeps coming back to it, and in her mouth the word takes on a moral coloration, and even an intense metaphysical value. But she has a very changeable image of it. The aspect she focuses on varies from moment to moment, depending on her mood. As if, by dreaming about it, she'd understood that it was not only a place of heat and solitude, but also a state of mind. Thus it appears to her sometimes as the place of mirages, of thirst, of emptiness, without age or landmarks, and sometimes, on the contrary, with the veiled shimmering of its light and the delicate vibrations of its silence, as the place of infinitely open spaces, of purity, of revelation. You have no idea what the source of this interest is. How should you respond to the questions she asks herself?

The desert again, with a new aspect. This time, what predominates is the image of the oasis sleeping in the calm of the night, when the sky and the stars, calming fears, favor reverie about limitless horizons. Faced with that, you don't dare repeat to her what Fabrice said: "What does all that bric-a-brac have to do with us? The true place of the oasis and palms is in mirages . . ."

Still this strange obsession with the Sahara. Tamara surprised you by speaking enthusiastically about the architecture of the M'zab, of these houses that are all alike, similar in their sobriety, which constitute the ksour of the Mozabites.[48] By what paths could her curiosity have led her there? You wonder if this is not a discreet way of flattering your exotic side, of helping you be proud of this part of you that you hardly ever show. For, even if you avoid mentioning this point in your little reports, she is still very interested in your person. She questions you, she rejoices, she worries. And you feel that she is, as usual, completely sincere.

Your visits are becoming less frequent. She asks you to write to her at greater length: "I want you to talk to me about yourself, nothing but yourself." A formula that often recurs in her letters. Up to this point, you've pretended not to hear. But you have written down these words, which you haven't dared say to her: "How can I talk to you about myself? Since your illness, it seems to me that I no longer have a self."

What has changed most, perhaps, is her relationship to her illness. Last year, she succeeded in not making any allusion to it, or only in an evasive, vague manner, by sighs and silences. You hardly noticed them, and it is only now that you grasp their meaning. She was trying, on the contrary, to tear away from life everything it could give: outings, readings. And these rendezvous in the Louvre she thought up! Enjoying a great freedom of movement, taking advantage of everyone's tendency to worship her, she succeeded in keeping her illness from occupying too much ground.

For your part, your denial of the situation was still more radical. Something in you simply didn't want to believe in the reality of this illness. When you happened to think of it, you didn't even manage to imagine the form it might have taken. All you put behind this word was a childishly purified image. You saw Tamara, wearing a particularly becoming look of languor and fragility on her face, spending her days reading and dreaming in an all-white room, on a large, lacquered armchair. Or else, when the morning sun was throwing its first squares of light on the wall, she went out to walk in the lanes of a large garden full of flowers and birds, gracefully breathing in the fragrance of freshly cut grass. Physical pain, the prosaic care that it requires, all that did not even occur to you.

Now, she knows that she is more seriously ill. She has lived through this long period, full of doctors, nurses, the smell of ether and disinfectant, as an exile, during which her sensibility has been exacerbated. So she hesitates less to talk about her condition. Without, however, going so far as to designate her illness, which remains for you mysterious. Cancer? leukemia? You hardly dare write these unutterable words.

You see Tamara passing through successive, contradictory states: sometimes moments of animation, almost of feverishness, her consciousness raised to the point of paroxysm; sometimes she seems tense, insidiously weakened, her internal harmony broken. What can all that mean?

It's clear that this admirable taste for life that so much attracted you is slowly changing. You see the tonality of her words, like that of her letters, occasionally turn toward a form of melancholy. But a sweet melancholy, consisting above all of distance, of detachment, without pride, from the things of ordinary life.

What if there were a relationship between her illness and your "story"? What if this mysterious illness was a way for her body to say what her mouth does not? It is to Fabrice, clearly surprised by the turn things have taken, to whom you owe this strange suggestion.

The desert has moved into the background. God, the soul, the infinite recur with increasing frequency in her remarks. As well as other words, just as unexpected: epiphany, Parousia. As if elevation of thought were connected with the progression of the physical malaise. A progression you don't see, but only divine.

She spoke for the first time of her nightmares: she sees things around her collapsing, monsters coming after her, sometimes, she says, she even forgets her own name . . .

You're discovering a Tamara profoundly imbued with belief, with religion. A subject she'd touched upon only briefly up to now. But this week, on several occasions, she quoted a remark, an anecdote, on the subject of a few Russian ascetics. Saint Dmitri of Rostov, Saint Seraphim of Sarov, the starets Zosima or the archimandrite Macarius. Personages wholly unknown to you, of course. You remember their names only because of their exoticism.

Concerning icons: moved, she talks to you about these faces with huge eyes, wasted by anxiety, or else about these silhouettes that seem cramped in a space without depth.

You imagine her in an attitude of prayer: kneeling, her hands joined, her head bowed, her eyes closed. Her beauty having become severe, even more pure. You try in vain to remember the great Italian paintings with which you wanted to identify her in this posture.

You note that she has a tendency to become absorbed in her internal sensations. You sense that in her, the moments of fear alternate with moments of joy, but you are unable to understand why. Sometimes, a shiver . . .

She seems increasingly ill at ease in her body, shot through by moments of fervor, elation, that make her want, she says, to detach herself from this world, to melt into the divine. All that surprises you, but it is beginning to have a kind of fascination for you.

How things have changed over the past few weeks! The other day, Tamara mentioned, spontaneously, the time of your first meetings, the discovery of your unexpected affinities, of your secret analogies. She grew sentimental over "the singular destiny of our friendship." The way she said that! The smile and the look . . . It's clear that this word was for her only a substitute, a pale ersatz for the one before which you have both always drawn back. Alas, there's no reason to rejoice in this. For she speaks in the past tense of this friendship with a singular destiny. There emanates from her words a feeling of "too late." Is it going to mark your relationship from now on?

You reproach yourself now for your blindness during the first months. Your excessive expectations had initially made of her, from the first glance, the perfect incarnation of "the girl." What for a long time gave you the courage to wait was that you'd discerned in her the moment when adolescent in-genuousness defends itself only reluctantly against the first assaults of desire, knowing full well that it will soon yield to them. Moreover, you insisted on seeing her only under the serene aspect she first presented to you. But you should have been more insightful. The ambiguities, the mysteries of her con-duct should have shown you the way. Should have made you understand that, in her relationship with you, she was living—go on, dare to say these words—a sort of spiritual drama.

20

Ellipsis

So now there you are, reader, transported into the middle of the month of May 1961. Yes, a great ellipsis in this chronicle, which up to this point adhered very closely to the university calendar. An ellipsis of more than a year. Connected, as you will have guessed, with an eclipse – of equal length – of Tamara. At the time of our exchange of letters during the preceding spring, she had informed me that she was going to have to leave Paris again. "Probably for several months." Without saying anything more. But I guessed her reasons. I was used to this now. And I even expected it a little: it was the third time that, in a strange reverse migration, she had flown away when summer approached.

I succeeded in not falling into the sadness and despair that had ruined the end of my preceding year: the conditions were not the same. This time, I had to devote myself entirely to my work. Not without difficulty, and with various phases of relapse, I succeeded in doing so. Fabrice's help, and also that of Michel and Gustave, were of great value to me. We took the examinations again and, luckily, all four of us passed. To celebrate the outcome, it remained for us only to complete what seemed to us one more rite of initiation, the last of an already long series of such rites: a trip to Greece. After which a new life, independent, free, and adult, could finally begin.

Feverishness, excitement, intensity of the first months spent in the Rue d'Ulm. The apparently infinite multiplicity of temptations, discoveries, encounters. Like many of those around me, taking care to exhaust – as we had been taught to do – the field of the possible, I devoured everything that turned up, sometimes even shoveling it in with both hands. There was so much lost time to make up!

A single dark point: all during this crucial period, Tamara, as she'd told me, continued to be absent. So I'd spent months and months without seeing her, without hearing the sound of her voice, without receiving any news of her. I'd sent her a note, of course, to tell her about my success, and then, from Greece, several postcards as well as a long letter. I didn't dare admit to her that the country I was traveling through hardly corresponded to the glorious place we used to talk about in the Louvre. However, hoping at least to make her smile, I mentioned the shores of the Ilissos, and even the slopes of Olympus and the Pindus range, to which my companions' reluctance had not allowed me to make a pilgrimage. I received no response.

Then (it's strange, but that's the way it is) her memory, almost in spite of myself, gradually became obscured by a slight veil. To be sure, my love for her was still there. An integral part of my being, a constitutive element of my person, there was no risk of its being erased! But it no longer had the violence that had so agitated, so tormented me. It now seemed to me discreet, restrained: it had taken on the sepia tints of the old photographs of my ancestors that, as a child, I liked to look at in the family album.

My active love life had taken an entirely different direction, an entirely different form. Completely free during the day and the night, constantly involved in the activities, distractions, and even, sometimes, little intrigues of the various groups I'd found it easy to join, I finally had an opportunity to look on women, on love, and on life in general, from a point of view somewhat less narrow, somewhat less anxious, than that of the transplanted schoolboy I'd been at first. There was no longer any question of confining myself to the idyllic dream whose vagaries had marked, for better and for worse, my three long years as a resident student at the Lycée. Without disowning that episode, without considering it closed, I felt the need for other experiences.

This was the period when I shamelessly indulged in a series of liaisons that lasted a night, a week, a month. The period when encounters with beautiful (and even, sometimes, not so beautiful, but only exciting) women I didn't know rarely went nowhere. A kind of behavior I tried to analyze. With, of course, the dose of pedantry that seemed to me required.

May 61. How to explain your current insatiable hunger? A hunger that led you, just last week, to look up, despite the interdict issued by Violetta, dear Francine, who was very surprised to be once again pulled away, for a few nights at least, from her solitary linguistic ecstasies. Your friends, except for Fabrice, who keeps stubbornly silent (a way of expressing his disapproval?), see in this, of course, only a compensating reaction after the long abstinence inflicted by Tamara. Michel and Gustave ironically attack you with erudition and witticisms.

"I read somewhere that Restif de la Bretonne divided his life into two parts: one pure and prudish, the other libertine, and even slightly obscene! Just like you . . ."

"Well, it was inevitable that you'd some day move from love as potentiality to love as act. And you think you're obliged to multiply these acts."

"As a result, if I dare say so, you've made quite a leap. You've jumped from frustration to provocation."

"Let's say rather from disappointment to defiance."

"A transitory crisis, and salutary to boot, my friend."

"Rejoice, you're in very good company. Mozart himself . . ."

"You don't remember? Because he couldn't have the woman he wanted, he amused himself by looking for women he didn't love. Solely for pleasure, for diversion."

"An attitude that you'll see again, in almost the same form, in Dominique, yes, Fromentin's hero."

"Well, then . . . In all these people, one way or another of masking a misogyny they find it hard to accept."

Despite their apparent plausibility, these explanations don't satisfy you. Too mechanical, too superficial. You're well aware of this: if you have to find a model for your present amorous behavior, it's certainly not in the direction of Don Juan that you'll look. Remaining in the Mozartian register, another figure would fit you much better, the brave and tender Cherubino. You, too, have the feeling that every woman makes your heart beat faster. If love is the turmoil elicited by beauty, why should it be limited to a single incarnation of beauty? But, mirabile dictu, these palpitations of your heart, instead of paralyzing you, now lead you to go all the way.

In fact, your attitude seems to proceed from a peculiarity of your character. Its origin should probably be sought in some obscure childhood trauma, but that's not your subject for the moment. This peculiarity consists in the fact that just as you cannot avoid having a heart pang when confronted by something that is coming to an end (how can one not see in it the prefiguration of other endings?), you dislike having to leave what has taken the place of company for you, even if only for a single evening. In a word, you find it hard to bear, and sometimes you cannot bear at all, what someone has called the bitterness of interrupted common feelings. You therefore find yourself almost always led, as soon as there is common feeling, to do everything you can to prevent its being interrupted. This is an impulse beyond your control, a sort of irresistible drive. You have to act on it immediately. Provoke a new encounter. Explore the road that has just opened before you. It can, it must lead to a form of tenderness, the very one you need at that moment. And despite the narrowness of the sample that you have contact with, since, from one rendezvous to another, you're almost always faced (you couldn't help bringing up this point!) with the same type of woman. But as soon as the thread is picked up again, you hasten to forget all your untimely sociological notions, and each of your new girlfriends becomes for you the singular, unique, indispensable being that you had immediately seen in her.

In the midst of this whirlwind of activity, Violetta, whom I had neglected a little since my return from Greece, but who seemed to be waiting for her chance, resurfaced. A very short letter, ironic and mocking ("So the Rue d'Ulm and its pomps have led you away from the path to Plaisance?"), urged me to come see her. I took a strange pleasure in going immediately to find her in the jumble of her studio, a jumble that had grown considerably since the last time I was there. My visit lasted no less than three days: the whole long Easter weekend. The embarrassment, even the guilt, I'd so strongly felt when we first resumed our relations, and which had already lessened in the course of our later meetings, had completely melted away.

Violetta had changed, though I was not quite sure why, for she remained discreet about her activities. The English lessons she'd begun taking no longer seemed to occupy much of her attention. I seemed to understand that she was traveling frequently, chiefly to Switzerland and Belgium. And also that she sometimes took in "young women in difficulty" or "North African friends who were passing through." I became better acquainted with her entourage: a swarm of buzzing young people (and a few others, less young, but just as buzzing, like the bearded prophet keen on sociology who scourged mass culture) excited to the point of intoxication by a tenacious desire for revolution. Among them, I made a few friends, whom I had the pleasure of meeting in the course of the little get-togethers, always more or less improvised, that she liked to organize at her place: a couple of bottles of gin or vodka, which someone agreed to bring along, a few liters of wine that someone went to buy, at the last minute, at the café in the Rue Pernéty, that's all it took. I was happy to invite Fabrice; I was finally going to be able to introduce him somewhere, to acquaint him with some new minds! He came with me several times, without assuming, as I had seen him do in other places, the resigned air of someone who has strayed into a group unworthy of him. It was even during one of these parties that he met Maria, with whom he was later to leave on a great expedition in northeastern Brazil.

Violetta agreed very gracefully to play with me the double role that, through force of circumstances, had become hers: an always-willing sex partner, occasionally combined with a big sister. She excelled in this, and was as necessary to me in one function as in the other. Even the extreme attitudes she liked to take sometimes, whether playfully or remaining faithful to her old provocations, no longer shocked me. I couldn't forget that she was the only person who had known intimately, and since my Moroccan years (so distant, now!), the successive phases of my evolution. The only one in whose arms I could find, beyond what she called disdainfully my Parisian escapades, the continuity of my life, and perhaps even a little, as she still liked to say, of my true identity. We were now strongly linked. By our more and more frequent and regular meetings. But also by the things we confided to each other, without concern about modesty, regarding the adventures that each of us considered ourselves expected to carry on independently. The distant memory of the *Liaisons dangereuses*, but also the model, closer at hand, of the Sartre-Beauvoir couple, which she had given me an opportunity to meet one evening, exercised their seductive force on us. I was astonished by her aptitude for moving, in her frequently stormy relationships with other men, from enthusiasm to sarcasm. She mocked, but without excessive irony, what she called my abrupt turnaround: "So you've ended up forgetting her, your evanescent Sylphide. It's about time!" she repeatedly told me. Without imagining that the too visible impatience of the senses had not dislodged in me the patience of the heart.

21

Promise

May 1961

Monday morning. Just after breakfast, which he'd eaten alone and in haste in the refectory – for he'd gotten up late after too short a night – Manuel had gone, as he did every day, to pick up his mail in his locker. The great vestibule of the École normale, where the wooden pigeonholes that served as mailboxes were arranged in columns, resounded with an unusual amount of activity, which he attributed to the sudden – and very welcome – return of good weather. He couldn't resist the desire to sit down on a bench in the sun, inside the internal garden that resembled a cloister, near the goldfish pond. A few laughing mathematics students, whom he greeted on the way, had preceded him.

Once he'd sat down, he began to sort through his packet of letters. He kept for later, in order to examine them at his leisure, a large envelope bearing a postmark from Sfax (he already had an idea of what it might contain), the new catalog of a publisher-bookseller on Rue Saint-Séverin, and some poorly duplicated tracts announcing a series of meetings/debates against the war in Algeria. The only letter he read, with an intense emotion – he had, of course, recognized the handwriting at first glance – was the one that contained a message from Tamara. The first in a year. Only a few lines. His friend, back "after a long, obligatory stay in the country" (without further explanation), offered him congratulations, regretting that they were so belated, on his success, which, she said, she had "never doubted." She thanked him for the cards and the messages sent from Greece; she would have so much liked to make as well this pilgrimage they had dreamed about together. Finally, she urged him not to allow himself to be eaten up by his new obligations, which she imagined to be "heavy and numerous," and to come back to see her very soon. A little surprised at first that she said not a word about her health, he concluded that everything must be going much better, that his friend was finally out of the woods. That was what he'd always hoped for: a miracle. A miracle that would cure her once and for all, and that would take them both back to their golden age. He hastened to reply that he was, as always, impatient to see her again, and that he would come by her home the following Sunday, in the early afternoon.

In fact, he was very sincerely happy about her return. He couldn't help hoping. He was delighted to note, once again, that time had not altered in her the sense of affinity that had so long bound them together, any more than it had attenuated, in him, his unsatisfied desire. Then why shouldn't there be a new start? But a lightning-fast start, this time. They were, the two of them, ready for a real adult love that would finally sweep away the slowness, the delays, the accumulated silences. Tamara, he was sure, was one of those people who have the courage to do anything, to risk anything, once they have consented to love. And moreover, what could she be risking now, with him? Without the slightest doubt, when they were finally together for good (soon, perhaps), they could both pride themselves – pointing to the meandering course of their story, that incredible succession of élans broken and constantly reborn – on not being, even for a moment, an ordinary couple!

When he rang her doorbell on Sunday, at the dot of two, he felt nervous and a little worried. In the entry hall where she had appeared to him for the first time, Tamara came to greet him, with a vivacity, a warmth, that sufficed to revive all his hopes. As soon as he was near her, she stretched her neck slightly to give him a sort of delicate kiss on his forehead, which he received with wondering surprise. Then she let her right hand, whose dampness he immediately felt, rest on him for moment, and did not withdraw it until they were both seated, as before, in their armchairs. Only then did he see the changes in his friend. She continued to smile at him, but her smile no longer succeeded in completely concealing her fatigue. A fragility, an unaccustomed pallor were written on her face. He was struck particularly by her eyes: they seemed to contain, in the brilliance of their light, most of her energy.

They talked for a long time, at first with increasing animation. She said nothing about her health, nothing about her reasons for being away, about her long silence (the longest since they had first met). He himself did not dare to question her on this subject, as if it were struck by a taboo that paralyzed him. She seemed instead to take pleasure in mentioning, one after another, in a disorder full of gaiety, what she called the highpoints of their friendship: their springtime laughter in the lanes of the Bois de Boulogne or the Luxembourg; the religious emotion they shared on the evenings spent at the TNP, their long pauses, punctuated by hushed discussions, in the ill-lit rooms of the Louvre, and, of course, their sessions of reading together. She even picked up, obviously moved, her big anthology with the worn binding. She opened it at random, and began to read, with a sort of veil in her voice:

La lune s'attristait. Des séraphins en pleurs
Rêvant, l'archet au doigt, dans le calme des fleurs.[49]

But she couldn't go beyond the fourth line,[50] and put the book back on the pedestal table, nervously pursing her lips in a way he'd never seen her do before. Her mother, who came into the room at that moment, offered to make them tea. They drank it in her company, and the conversation among the three of them, around the little silver samovar, concerned chiefly life at the École normale. As he was leaving, he held his friend in his arms for a brief moment, promising, that as she suggested, he would return the following week at the same time.

He returned in fact, and they resumed talking about their memories, as if the weight of all that past was clearly less difficult for them to bear than that of the present. And then suddenly, without any transition, in a monotone, she began to tell him about the boredom of her days of confinement, the past winter, when she was not permitted anything in her clinic in the Vosges, not even a novel. Of the last things they said to each other, he remembered only one sentence, uttered with suppressed vehemence: "Manuel, you'll have to help me get out of the dungeon, quickly."

He returned to her home twice, on consecutive Sundays. The first time, he was met by Tamara's mother, the second by Sonia. Without telling him anything about his friend's condition, they both seemed to him much less relaxed than usual. The last time they met, he couldn't help noticing his friend's diaphanous face, as if it were lit from within by suffering. He was not surprised when she asked him to suspend his visits for a while.

"I'll miss you, too, as you know very well. But it's for only a week or two. No longer. I promise you, Manuel. Yes, I promise you."

22

Image

It's a Friday evening, at the beginning of June 1961. It's still light outside, and a summer mildness envelops the old building along the Rue d'Ulm. Accompanied by Gustave, Manuel has just come back from the lecture on Homeric philology at the Sorbonne, the last one of the year. On the way, he gives a routine glance at his locker. A *pneumatique* has been put in it during the afternoon. "Tamara!" he says to himself, delighted. And he quickly thrusts his hand into the narrow pigeonhole to get the letter. Still lighter than usual, it seems. Almost diaphanous. The handwriting is Sonia's. "Hmm, it's been months since she's written me . . ."

She asks him to call her right away at Rue Nicolo, it's an emergency.

He hurries toward the dirty nook that serves as a telephone booth for the students at the École normale. A miracle: the phone is free. With a trembling finger, Manuel dials the number. Gets a wrong number. Tries again.

Sonia's voice at the other end of the line. Unrecognizable. Broken words. Over and over, he has to ask her to repeat what she's said. She mumbles. He still doesn't understand. Between two sobs, she finally manages to tell him the news.

"Tamara, yes, Tamara . . . She's dead. Yes, dead. Last night, yes. And yet, for three or four days she'd been saying she felt better . . . She asked me several times to let you know . . . Yes, she thought she might be able to see you next Sunday . . ."

Stupor. Incredulity. Pain. His mind is completely filled by incoherent words. Absurd. Scandalous. Unjustifiable. While he's writing down, on the back of the wrinkled letter he's still holding, details about the hour and location of the funeral mass, tears are flowing.

He doesn't have the strength to wipe them away. Gustave, standing near him, assumes a fitting expression and remains silent.

Three days afterward, as hesitating and awkward as a sick person, Manuel went into an unfamiliar church, somewhere in the north part of Paris, near the Rue de Crimée. Violetta, at whose place he'd ended up taking refuge after two sleepless nights, had insisted on taking him, in her old 2cv, as far as the door of the building.

He had hardly taken a few steps in the half-light when he felt himself enveloped by a strange bouquet of odors, which immediately revived the memory of other places. A few chapels he'd visited in the mountains of Greece, during his trip the past summer. But especially the great church on Rue Daru where, in order to feel himself in communion with Tamara, who had been out of town for months, he'd gone to walk around the preceding year, on the occasion of the Orthodox Easter. He'd discovered there an unknown world, inspiring and exotic: the profusion of icons, carpets, and chandeliers, the pathos of the songs, the solemnity of the ritual, the odor, so strong, of incense and wax, everything had impressed him and he'd promised himself to go back there someday, as soon as possible, with her; she alone would be able to explain the mysteries of this religion to him.

He moved slowly toward the altar, around which a small group had gathered. Only women: Tamara's mother, her aunts, her cousins. He'd met all of them over the past three years. But in their mourning clothes, he hardly recognized them. As soon as she saw him, Sonia took a few steps toward him and embraced him for a long time. Then, without a word, holding him by the hand, she led him toward the little family unit that opened to make room for him and then closed again immediately.

A few steps from there, just at the corner of the altar, four men in black had come to set down, with gestures full of solemnity, a casket of light-colored oak: the brand-new brass plaque bore Tamara's name, as well as the two dates that marked the limits between which the few years of her life had taken place. Long minutes passed in complete silence.

Suddenly, a choir that couldn't be seen and that seemed composed solely of masculine voices began a long series of psalmodies. From them emerged, with a frequency that quickly became obsessive, a few groups of syllables, the only ones Manuel was capable of recognizing, because they had long been familiar to him: those of the word "Gospodin," uttered in an imploring tone, those of the word "Alleluia," which seemed to fly from mouth to mouth among the invisible singers, constantly repeated, indefinitely modulated, in countless poignant ways. The tears Manuel had been trying to suppress since he entered the church then overwhelmed him.

It was only after a long moment of emptiness, and of a sort of paralysis, that his mind began to function again. Through his pain, one or two thoughts, which had pushed aside all the others, kept coming back. Could he forget that one of Tamara's last concerns, one of her last plans, had been about him, about seeing him? He told himself that he clearly owed a great deal, almost everything, to this unique being that Providence had sent him: she had appeared at exactly the right time, and since her first apparition, had never left him again, bringing him, wherever she was and whatever she was doing, the only intense moments of his life. He also told himself that if Tamara had died a few months earlier, in those days when his love for her was constantly devouring him, he would probably have lost all desire to live on: the temptation would have been great to rejoin his friend, not to try, like Orpheus, to bring her back to this world which had hardly known how to accommodate their love, but in order to merge with her and finally to constitute, with her, that being with a double body of which he had so often dreamed.

At the same time, he couldn't help asking himself what his friend's last moments were like. Letting his imagination run free, he was assailed by contradictory visions. Some of them were unbearable: the eyes closed forever, the ice-cold hands, the heart that no longer beat, the naked body . . . He pushed them away with irritation. Along with those that, however little, suggested the death agony, the malfunctioning of the organs, the degradation of the body. He wanted to retain only those that seemed to him noble. No, he could testify to it because he had seen her only a few days before, Tamara had been carried off in the flower of her youth. Without ugliness, without stain of any kind. Nothing macabre. Nothing funereal. Just a somewhat accentuated fever and pallor. He was anxious to guarantee her in this way the privilege of a beautiful death, one that, like that of warriors of yore who fell in the prime of life, gives the right to survive in human memory. For she must have fought terrible battles before succumbing in this way . . .

But he was also anxious to determine his own role in this sadly lost battle. What errors could he have committed? At what points? He felt guilty for all the daring he hadn't had. Hadn't he been, with his prudishness and procrastination, his slowness and his blindness, one of the instruments of destiny? The one that had allowed such an unfinished idyll to end in tragedy.

At times, in spite of himself, his reverie went off in other, more vertiginous directions. Perhaps by trying to exonerate himself of part of his responsibilities, he wanted to forget the tragedy, to situate this death, on the contrary, in a logic of a completely different order. There came back to him in fragments the philosophy classes he'd taken, those formulas about Eros and love that had then appeared so pompous, so ridiculous. It seemed to him that he now understood them better. What if Tamara had appeared only to represent, in the eyes of everyone who had come near her, the ideal, around which we turn without being able to attain it? Or else the absolute, which one approaches without being able to possess it? Then he could console himself for the scandal of her death, consider it as a reward that had come to crown, at exactly the right time, the mission of an exceptional being. An apotheosis, in short.

And, whereas the Orthodox ritual, always accompanied in the background by the psalmodies of the invisible choir, unfolded its majestic sadness in the half-light, he promised himself inwardly that he would do everything ("from now on, it will be your permanent concern, the secret heart of your activity as a survivor"), yes, to do everything ("and what does it matter if this responsibility should prove to be heavy to bear") to give his dead young friend the immortality of heroines and martyrs. He would preserve, as relics, the slightest traces that came to him from her. But above all, he would celebrate her. He would try to invent the words and the sentences that would restore to her the plenitude of life: her gestures, her walk, her perfume, her remarks, and even the timbre of her voice. At the same time, he would see to it that she became, for all those who would come to know her only through him, a myth. The myth that she had already become, from that instant forward, for him.

Suddenly, he perceived that people were moving about in the church. The ceremony had just ended, with a final alleluia, still more heart-rending than all the others. The little group of women in black had broken up. Some of them came toward him to embrace him. He had no difficulty in recognizing Sophie, of course, and the big, beautiful green eyes of Tatiana. The others . . . All around him, people were weeping, embracing each other, exchanging words in Russian that made their sobs redouble. Then came a moment when Tamara's mother, seeing that he was alone, took him by the arm and led him away, murmuring in his ear words he did not understand.

In the black-draped hearse that was to take the little family group to the place of interment, he found himself squeezed between Sophie and Tatiana. Suddenly it grew warm. The trip seemed to him very long, punctuated by Sonia's nervous sobs. From time to time, Sophie and Tatiana said a few anodyne words: the efforts they were making to lighten the atmosphere fell flat. Manuel, sweating in his black jacket, hardly dared open his mouth. He asked, regarding the life and death of his friend, none of the questions that were, much later on, to trouble him so much.

When the little convoy finally arrived at Sainte-Geneviève-des-Bois, everything seemed to him to go much too fast. There were not many of them in the cemetery. Following the instructions of a tall man in a black suit, they formed a circle around a freshly dug grave. The coffin was effortlessly lowered into the grave, in a silence broken only by a few birds' cries. A brief ray of sun came to play, one last time, on the shiny brass plaque. Manuel immediately knew that this image would never be erased from his memory.

The Green Notebook

What should I do with my new notebook, the most recent of the useful gifts my aunt is fond of? A diary, perhaps? I remember that I began one, the first and only one up to now, when I was about ten years old. It was a very small notebook with a black cover. In it, I carefully wrote the names of all my dolls. I amused myself, with Sonia's help, in giving them all double or triple names. Forenames we thought very chic: Marinette, Adelaide, Rosalie, Isadora, Noémie, Anastasia . . . I also wrote down the occasion on which each one had been given me. Not much else, it seems to me. But wait a minute! I remember that I added a pencil mark, a very small black cross, before the names of those that got broken. Since those distant times, nothing. It's that I don't much like the idea of keeping a diary. It's too much like a "girl," or even a girl from a "good family"! And at this moment everything that seems like a "girl" revolts me. Why? Good question. But it would take at least a full page of my diary to answer it. And since I especially don't want to keep a diary . . . There, I've come full circle.

So. I'm going to say instead that this is my commonplace book. One of those "readings notebooks" that people liked to put together in the last century (dixit my dear aunt). It will be my treasury, amassed line by line. I will come to draw on it later on, according to my needs. But if there are quotations that awaken an idea (and necessarily, there will be), well, I'll write that down too. Simple, isn't it? So I can begin. In fact, I've already begun. My pirouettes the other night at least allowed me to start.

Today I'm taking, in Stendhal (he's inevitable, alas!), my first lesson in love. At almost seventeen, it's about time! In fact, I've not yet found much, except this: "The emptiness of a great soul can be fulfilled only by a being." Beautiful, isn't it?

A short detour via Michelet: "What harangue delivered by a man will equal the effect of a woman's silence?" (*L'Amour*, I, 1, toward the end).

A woman's silence! There's a problem that hardly concerns you, my dear Sonia, does it? But it does me. For a long time, I kept quiet. I mistrusted words. I suspected them of wanting to substitute themselves, insidiously, for being. I was wrong. No, words don't shackle being.

If I kept quiet, if words did not come to me spontaneously, that was because a sort of fear paralyzed me. But what do I have to talk about, now that I've acceded to language? Nothing but this emptiness I find deep inside me and that I don't know how to fill.

Sonia has recently begun a friendship with a boy to whom, if I understood correctly, she wrote without knowing him. That seems to work for her.

Sonia's friend. His black, black curls. His eyes. His hands, too. No, I wasn't afraid when I saw his eyes, as if dazzled, resting on me, from the first moment. On the contrary. Even the metro car, which gaily got involved by throwing us together. I like those signs.

His silence in the theater. He seemed so tense, so uneasy. Why did I decide I should run away? Well, anyway, I think we'll see each other again. But things mustn't be rushed.

Picked up in Balzac (*Eugénie Grandet*):
"If light is the first love of our lives, isn't love the first light of our hearts?"
"Reserve, or rather timidity, is one of the first virtues of love."

Him, again. I'm not sure I really like his first name, which I prefer not to write. His silence, like the last time. But now, he knows that I will always be there. Perhaps someday we'll refer to that rainy Sunday as that of the "Pact of the Tuileries."

Certain feelings are born in their plenitude and don't need to mature. I don't remember where I found that. No time to check. I'm sure Manuel knows. Do I have the courage to ask him? No, of course not.

He resembles me like a brother. If only he were really my brother (the way he says "Ariane, my sister . . .").

Valéry: "In this world, everything can be born from an infinite waiting" (La jeune Parque).

How should I answer Sonia, who has asked me several times, with increasing starchiness, why I'm writing this "diary" (a question I hadn't really asked myself, except perhaps on the first day). Like this, perhaps: a little of my truth has to be expressed somewhere. Moreover, I maintain that this is not a true diary. The proof is that there isn't a single concrete fact, not a single date. I will adhere to this rule.

Blessed ambiguity of words. Now, Manuel is my "friend," and I am his "friend." No one finds anything to object to in this declared friendship. If only that lasts!

The well-behaved liturgy of our meetings. Week after week, now. I love the old-fashioned preciousness that comes over his language, sometimes. His sentences, always a little too careful, just as his handwriting is too small.

Our walks around Paris. I'd like none of them to happen from now on without being for us the occasion for at least one moment that is unforgettable because it is unique, absolute.

"A soul that has met by chance a body and that manages as best it can." That, which I understand only too well, was said about a certain Joubert (a philosopher, I believe).

Piaf concert: all those songs that seem finally to meld into one. Yes, a single one, in which a single verb is conjugated. In all its tenses, in all its modes, in all its persons. The verb "to love," of course.

But what initiatives should I take? What gestures? What words should I say? Too heavy a responsibility.

And all those signs that above all I don't want to see ...

"Asymptote": there's something in this word that pleases me and frightens me.

In what does it consist, then, this happiness that people talk about so much, in books and elsewhere? The apparent simplicity of other people's "loves," mediocre. I would like to be capable of rejecting the slightest gesture, the slightest word, that might lead our friendship toward a passing infatuation.

I know I'm full of contradictions. What can I do about it? The world is contradictory too: it contains the dry and the moist, the cold and the hot, the calm and the tempest ...

Still another contradiction: the double meaning of the word "grace"!

Sailing an uncertain course among the heroines of his favorite novels. With which one should I identify? Mustn't choose the wrong novel! One thing is sure, at least: neither Mme Bovary nor Mme de Rênal. But I seem a little young to be Mme Arnoux. As for Mme de Mortsauf ...[51]

We are really in agreement. There is only one thing worthwhile in the cosmogonies invented by our cherished Hellenes: the place they give to the forces to which the gods themselves are subject. A way of excusing in advance some of our own weaknesses, poor mortals?

Respond clearly to his love one of these days? Maybe. Maybe even by going beyond it . . . Don't forget that "the first symptom of true love in a young man is timidity, whereas in a young woman, it is boldness" (V. Hugo, *Les Misérables*, IV, III, 6).

> Et pour qui, dévorée
> D'angoisses, gardez-vous la splendeur ignorée
> Et le mystère vain de votre être?[52]
> MALLARMÉ (HÉRODIADE)

Ah, poets sometimes ask such questions!

Yes, of course, I'm close to you. Very close. Closer than you've ever been able to believe. And even, sometimes, I feel identical to you. But that is in a region of myself that I prefer for the moment not to know. So I won't say anything to you. You also have to know how to guess sometimes!

Guess . . . Alas, it seems to me sometimes that we all lack an eye, an ear, a sense through which we could know other aspects of ourselves and others.

We girls don't go into the world. It's the world that goes into us. And with what violence, sometimes.

But I'm talking here about something I don't yet know. Something I shall perhaps never know.

About violence, precisely:

"The violence one does oneself in order to prevent oneself from loving is often crueler than the rigors of what one loves" (La Rochefoucauld, *Maximes*, 369).

"Virtue, in all the flower of its silliness."

That's in *Le Père Goriot*. It doesn't make me laugh . . .

"It is more difficult to get along without kisses than without words," Heinrich Heine is supposed to have written at the end of his life. At the end of his life . . . I might not have that much patience.

Is moderation always a virtue? Sounds like the topic of an essay assignment . . . But I have really asked myself the question. Provisional response: before taking refuge in moderation, one should first have had at least a taste of excess.

I find these lines in the first pages of the *Secrets de la princesse de Cadignan*, and I take a certain pleasure in copying them out here:

" '. . . a young man [. . .] looking at me with fire in his eyes, but often saddened by the distance he sees between us, or perhaps also by the impossibility of succeeding.'

" 'Poor boy! When one is in love, one becomes very silly,' the marquise said."

A little farther on:

"Love, for inferior beings a simple need of the senses, [is] for superior beings the most immense and most engaging moral creation."

And almost at the end, when the princess "places a saintly kiss on the forehead" of Arthez:

" 'Oh, you illustrious fool! Don't you see that I'm madly in love with you?"

A princess's way of behaving. According to the family chronicle, there was a time – not so long ago – when we were princesses too. Become one again?

Cries of passion, cries of distress. Who can know the sufferings I endure? An old feminine refrain. And what if this secret wound were only the sign, the annunciation of mercies to come?

"Love feeds on starvation and dies from being fed." Who could have thought, written that?

Why did I suddenly feel the need to read *The Idiot*? (I'm honest, I didn't say "reread.")

Revolted this evening by the sweet Myshkin's reply to Rogozhin: "Do you know that there are women who torture a man through cruelty and sarcasm, without the least scruple, because every time they look at him they say to themselves: 'At this moment, I am torturing him, but I will pay him back through love.'"

Women poets. Some of them find strange expressions that scare me. My harvest today, in a poetess named Andrée Vernay: "Desire: a sphinx crowned with rapacious claws." Or again: "Love is pinned to humanity."

What should I do with my body? I fear the moment when I am going to feel that tenseness that starts in the neck and rapidly spreads to the temples. I know that in this way it heralds the arrival of something stronger, more worrisome and delightful at the same time.

Flee the image, even the idea of my desire. Or else bury it, as deeply as possible. Above all, don't name it, as you have just done, you silly girl!

Hospital: Like another life in a closed world, in a parallel universe. Let's hope it won't last.

No one has said anything to me about the reasons that have brought me here. And probably no one will tell me anything. It seems simply that my "condition" (elevated pulse, palpitations) requires "long-term treatment" . . .

I'm repeatedly told that I must be courageous, that I'm going to have to fight. But I'm sure that I'd fight my illness far better if I could first understand it, name it.

Time, blocked.

I'm going to have to learn to fill the voids this separation has created. With what? My only consolation: the sounds of nature, the trees. Some of them are still in bloom. A little while ago, picked up a hawthorn branch that had broken off. It seems to me that by listening closely, I could hear them breathe.

The other day, on a completely white branch, carved with evident care, two initials, closely interlaced. A little wink from destiny, certainly. All that was lacking was the cooing of lovebirds . . .

The clouds this morning: they were slowly getting longer, in increasingly slender threads.

I find new smells everywhere here. Rimbaud gave colors to vowels. For me, they would have smells instead. Tastes?

This strange border that separates things one thinks from those one writes. And yet, that's not true! Even to language I don't want to entrust anything that passes through me at times. Since I have known that I was double, words have become objects of mistrust again: my suffering is accompanied by the impossibility of expressing it.

A real conspiracy: all these love novels that fill the shelves of libraries and booksellers, but not a one, it seems, that has foreseen a case like mine! What is literature good for, then?

The worst thing here: this acceptance of a routine that gradually substitutes itself for our individual will. Only my mental state changes from day to day, from hour to hour.

So many words, and such learned ones, in our letters. To hide our silence on the essential point. But who is fooled by this, really? I'm afraid our whole correspondence is only a sort of mirage: each of us is ultimately writing only for himself.

The Louvre, our palace. While waiting for the banks of the Scamander or the slopes of Mt. Ida.

This taste for voluptuousness that we have in common. In painting . . .

Why are we so much at ease amid all these immobile beauties, caught in a single gesture, a single attitude, and as if frozen on their bit of canvas?

An aesthetic bias that becomes paralyzing, in the long run!

Pernette du Guillet and Maurice Scève: friends, not lovers . . . And they are not the first ones in the series! Test? Sacrifice? Transcendence? Asceticism? In her, in any case, a sort of voluptuousness of sadness, drawn precisely from sacrifice . . . She writes:

Quand vous me voyez toujours celle
Qui pour vous souffre et son mal cèle
Me laissant par lui consumer
Ne me devez-vous bien aimer?
[. . .]
Qui dira que t'ai révélé
Le feu longtemps en moi celé
Pour en toi voir si force il a:
Je ne sais rien moins que cela.[53]

What should I say about the present state of my "inner life"? I've begun to make for myself what I call an "anti-credo." Here are some of its first articles:

    1. I do not believe that living is a sin.
    2. I do not believe that God likes my suffering.
    3. Nor that he needs it. What would he do with it?
    That, I do not want to believe, I don't want to believe it (and it is I, Tamara, who repeats and who underlines!).

We are both doing all we can to keep our desire from being realized. Perhaps we're afraid of being disappointed?

All these abandoned lovers: Ariane, Phaedra, Medea, Dido . . . Alarming, isn't it? Which one of them, then, gave her lover the impression that he'd become a burden?

"Every illness is love metamorphosed" (Thomas Mann). What if it were true?

Write to him. Write to him something other than my usual sooth-ing chitchat. Tell him calmly, serenely, the reasons for my attitude. What future is there for us? After the elation of the first moments, and despite the kinship of our souls, our differences will soon re-appear.

The feeling of my fragility, the source of my renunciation.

On one hand, I voluntarily restrain my love in order not to have to suffer from it (he knows this: we talked one day about the Prin-cess of Cleves . . .).[54] On the other hand, I don't want to inflict an unbearable suffering on him, either.

Rule: when death looms (who knows whether this is the case?), don't give yourself to a man you thereby risk making miserable. But how to tell him that?

Talk to him as well about my tendencies toward mysticism. Re-cently discovered. Right here. In my confinement.

Mallarmé's swan, trapped in a frozen pond.

Salt is never whiter than in Massawa, in Eritrea, on the shores of the Red Sea. Why have I been, for three days now, hounded by this sentence? Where does it come from? What is it telling me?

The desert, in order to flee desire . . . My rejection of the concrete, of the flesh, of the world, can only grow. At times, it's as if all that had already left me.

About my illness. I don't know its true nature. But I see clearly its development. Why should I multiply hypotheses? One thing is cer-tain: I will no longer be the same when I get out of here. I'm angry at my body for having let me down like this.

All these places to which illness has taken me. All these people with whom it has forced me to associate. And especially, all these days missed, literally thrown overboard. As if time were disappearing.

I know what I want to do when I get out of here, when I leave my little hell saturated with whiteness: plunge with exhilaration into that marvelous and distant realm, the external world. Yes, the streets, the cafés, the buses, the movie houses, the shops. People who enjoy them every day don't know their value.

Physical pain has at least this advantage over the other kind: one forgets it as soon as it stops.

Manuel, I'd like to be able to write you long letters, but I don't have that kind of daring or simplicity.

I'm afraid of boring you, and then we'd have to get used to each other again and freely open the portals of our minds and hearts. Without doing that, it's very hard.

Nothing can any longer stop me from being lucid: I'm well aware that ultimately I'll have to give in. What's tragic is discovering that the cause in which one believed is an illusion.

"Nothing that is not God can meet my expectation" (Pascal).

"God's speech is silence. The secret speech of God's love cannot be anything other than silence" (Simone Weil).

Notes

1. A reference to Michel Leiris's preface to his autobiographical book *L'Âge d'homme*.
2. The Lycée class that prepares students for the prestigious École normale supérieure.
3. The first three appear in Victor Hugo's *Les Misérables*, the latter in Anatole France's *Le Petit Pierre*.
4. *L'Equipe* is a daily newspaper devoted to sports.
5. *Bicas* are students who have failed the entrance examination twice and are preparing for a third attempt.
6. *Bizut* is student slang for a first-year student.
7. Maurice Blanchot, a contemporary critic and philosopher.
8. André Breton, a French surrealist poet and theoretician.
9. *L'Humanité* is the newspaper published by the French Communist Party.
10. *Pistons* are students preparing for the entrance examination for the École centrale.
11. *Colos* are students preparing for the entrance examination for the École coloniale.
12. "Good sister."
13. Allusions to Marcel Proust's *Swann in Love*, Johann Wolfgang von Goethe's *The Apprenticeship of Wilhelm Meister* and *The Sufferings of Young Werther*, and Robert Musil's *The Confusions of Young Törless*.
14. There is here an untranslatable play on *connaisse* and *méconnaisse*; the latter word sounds like "Meknès," the city in Morocco where the author was born.
15. "Will these promises, these perfumes, these infinite kisses / Be reborn from an unfathomable abyss?"
16. "The nine portals of your body."
17. *Les Temps modernes* was a prestigious journal founded by Jean-Paul Sartre; Vladimir Jankélévitch was a French philosopher; Fabrice Del Dongo is the hero of Stendhal's novel *La Chartreuse de Parme*; "le grand Meaulnes" is the eponymous hero of a novel (1913) by Alain-Fournier.

18. A neighborhood in Paris (8th arrondissement), where the apartment building described in Georges Perec's *La Vie mode d'emploi* is supposed to be located.
19. See Arthur Rimbaud's poem, "Le Bateau ivre."
20. By Jean de La Fontaine.
21. "La grosse Gégène" was the name given to the electrical generator used by the French army to torture Algerian prisoners during the Algerian War (1954-61).
22. A message sent in a capsule through a system of tubing running throughout Paris.
23. An obstreperous character in Hergé's Tintin comic book series.
24. Théâtre National Populaire, a theater founded in 1920 to bring theater to the general public, and directed in the 1950s by the celebrated actor/director Jean Vilar.
25. The *carte du Tendre* is a famous seventeenth-century "map of the land of love," which first appeared in Mme de Scudéry's novel *Clélie* (1654-1660).
26. An allusion to Paul Valéry's poem "La Jeune Parque."
27. The heroes of Gustave Flaubert's *Education sentimentale* (Frédéric), Stendhal's *Le Rouge et le noir* (Julien), and Honoré Balzac's *Le Lys dans la vallée* (Félix). The references to Mme Arnoux, Mme de Rênal, and Mme de Mortsauf a few lines farther on are to the heroines of these same novels, respectively.
28. "On your young breast, which whiteness defends / Let my head roll, attached to its prey." An amalgam of verses taken from Paul Verlaine, Stephane Mallarmé, and Jean Racine.
29. See Valery Larbaud, *Fermina Marquez*, chap. 14.
30. "Flowers are words of love / Words more tender than a poem."
31. In French, the difference between *réel* (reality) and *rêve* (dream).
32. Escort.
33. The Institut d'Études Politiques.
34. The École normale supérieure.
35. Lit., "The tranquil cenobites," but in French this is homophonic with "laissez nos bites tranquilles" ("leave our pricks alone").
36. *La Nouvelle Héloïse* is an epistolary novel by J. J. Rousseau (1761) whose title recalls the love of Abelard and Heloise.
37. In ancient Rome, criminals sentenced to death were hurled from Tarpeian rock.
38. Members of the Compagnies républicaines de sécurité, a national police force charged with maintaining public order, and known for its severity.

39. *Délie* is a cycle of 449 ten-line love poems by Maurice Scève (1544).

40. A figure immortalized in Alain Chartier's poem of the same title (fifteenth century).

41. "Everyone is borne by his own pleasure."

42. *La philosophie dans le boudoir* (1795), by the Marquis de Sade.

43. "Get drunk" (*Le Spleen de Paris*, XXXIII).

44. "I love the memory of those nude periods," "Whose statues Phoebus took pleasure in gilding." See Charles Baudelaire, *Fleurs du mal, V.*

45. See Baudelaire, *Fleurs du mal, II.*

46. "The book and its author played the role of Galahad." Galahad, in fact, is the knight who facilitated the love of Lancelot and Guinevere, King Arthur's wife. [Author's note.]

47. I.e., they had decided not to prepare themselves for the entrance examination for the École normale supérieure, but had enrolled in the Sorbonne instead.

48. Ksour (plural of the Arabic word *ksar*) are fortified villages located in oases in the Sahara; the Mozabites or M'zabites are the inhabitants of the M'zab, a group of oases in northern part of the Algerian Sahara.

49. "The moon was growing sad. Seraphim in tears / Dreaming, their bows on their fingers, in the calm of the flowers." Mallarmé, "Apparition."

50. The fifth line of Mallarmé's poem reads: "C'était le jour béni de ton premier baiser" ("It was the blessed day of your first kiss").

51. See note 27 above.

52. "And for whom, devoured / By fears, are you keeping the unknown splendor / And empty mystery of your being?"

53. "When you see me always the one / Who suffers for you and hides her pain / Letting myself be consumed by it / Mustn't you love me well? / [. . .] / Which will tell you that I have revealed / The fire long hidden within me / To see if in you it has power: / I know nothing less than that."

54. An allusion to the eponymous heroine of a novel by Mme de Lafayette (1679).